The Balkans
in World History

The
New
Oxford
World
History

The Balkans in World History

Andrew Baruch Wachtel

OXFORD

UNIVERSITY PRESS

2008

OXFORD
UNIVERSITY PRESS

Oxford University Press, Inc., publishes works that further
Oxford University's objective of excellence
in research, scholarship, and education.

Oxford New York
Auckland Cape Town Dar es Salaam Hong Kong Karachi
Kuala Lumpur Madrid Melbourne Mexico City Nairobi
New Delhi Shanghai Taipei Toronto

With offices in
Argentina Austria Brazil Chile Czech Republic France Greece
Guatemala Hungary Italy Japan Poland Portugal Singapore
South Korea Switzerland Thailand Turkey Ukraine Vietnam

Published by Oxford University Press, Inc.
198 Madison Avenue, New York, New York 10016

www.oup.com

Oxford is a registered trademark of Oxford University Press

Library of Congress Cataloging-in-Publication Data
Wachtel, Andrew.
The Balkans in world history / Andrew Baruch Wachtel.
p. cm.
Includes bibliographical references and index.
ISBN 978-0-19-515849-6; 978-0-19-533801-0 (pbk.)
1. Balkan Peninsula—History. 2. Europe, Eastern—History. I. Title.
DR36.W33 2008
949.6—dc22   2008015134

Printed in the United States of America
on acid-free paper

*Frontispiece: Slavic peasant women, still spinning thread in
the ancient Roman method in 1937.*
Library of Congress LC-USZ62–68247

Contents

Editors' Preface vii

Introduction: The Balkans as
Borderland and Melting Pot 1

CHAPTER 1   Beginnings: From Prehistory
to the Byzantine Empire. 11

CHAPTER 2   The Medieval Balkans 29

CHAPTER 3   The Balkans under Ottoman Rule. 51

CHAPTER 4   The Long Nineteenth Century (1775–1922). 72

CHAPTER 5   The Twentieth Century:
From the Balkans to Southeast Europe. 97

Chronology 127

Notes. 131

Further Reading. 133

Web Sites. 137

Acknowledgments 139

Index 141

Contents

Editors' Preface

The region known as the Balkans has long been a crossroads of the world. Traders, armies, messengers, and migrating tribes traveled the Balkans' varied landscape pursuing their livelihoods or searching for land on which to settle. Peoples of many ethnicities—Slavs, Greeks, Turks, Germans, Gypsies, and many others—layered their cultures atop one another as they set up residences and intermingled. As a result, these diverse inhabitants of the Balkans often spoke multiple languages in order to communicate with neighbors and the wanderers or invaders who traversed their lands. Kings in medieval times established multiethnic states, making the Balkans a model for the ways in which dynasties (and in the twentieth century, determined rulers such as Marshal Tito of Yugoslavia) could meld ethnicities rather than pit them against one another.

Imitating the splendor of Constantinople, Balkan rulers built lavish palaces and well-adorned places of worship. Rulership passed among the differing ethnicities and faiths, but most residents of the region did not care, worrying only who was in charge locally and how high the local lord would make taxes. Under Ottoman rule, prior to 1914, the capital at Constantinople dictated a policy of religious and cultural toleration so long as citizens paid their taxes and were willing to surrender some of their sons to be trained for the Ottoman armies. Complexity of peoples and cultures was a major characteristic of Balkan life for hundreds of years—which is not to say there were not tensions and even violent disagreements.

This layered society came under the influence of the great powers in the nineteenth century, as intellectuals and nationalist politicians sought to import the idea of the nation-state to their region. For their part the great powers were only too happy to interfere in Balkan affairs, with an eye to the advantages that restructuring of the region could bring to their own empires, which were crucially connected to the eastern Mediterranean. As the nationalist ideal took hold, in 1914 a nationalist youth, Gavrilo Princip, ignited World War I by assassinating an heir to Balkan territories so that he might free his homeland. In the aftermath of the devastation wrought by that war, Balkan politicians succeeded in dividing their region into distinct nation-states, among them the state of Yugoslavia. These states struggled with problems of multiple ethnicities in an age of ethnically based nation-states and great power influence after World War I, during the period of Communist domination through the 1990s, and even in the post–Cold War era. It is a complex and sometimes tragic story.

This book is part of the New Oxford World History, an innovative series that offers readers an informed, lively, and up-to-date history of the world and its people that represents a significant change from the "old" world history. Only a few years ago, world history generally amounted to a history of the West—Europe and the United States—with small amounts of information from the rest of the world. Some versions of the old world history drew attention to every part of the world *except* Europe and the United States. Readers of that kind of world history could get the impression that somehow the rest of the world was made up of exotic people who had strange customs and spoke difficult languages. Still another kind of "old" world history presented the story of areas or peoples of the world by focusing primarily on the achievements of great civilizations. One learned of great buildings, influential world religions, and mighty rulers but little of ordinary people or more general economic and social patterns. Interactions among the world's peoples were often told from only one perspective.

This series tells world history differently. First, it is comprehensive, covering all countries and regions of the world and investigating the total human experience—even those of so-called peoples without histories living far from the great civilizations. "New" world historians thus share in common an interest in all of human history, even going back millions of years before there were written human records. A few "new" world histories even extend their focus to the entire universe, a "big history" perspective that dramatically shifts the beginning of the story back to the Big Bang. Some see the "new" global framework of world history today as viewing the world from the vantage point of the moon, as one scholar put it. We agree. But we also want to take a close-up view, analyzing and reconstructing the significant experiences of all of humanity.

This is not to say that everything that has happened everywhere and in all time periods can be recovered or is worth knowing, but that there is much to be gained by considering both the separate and interrelated stories of different societies and cultures. Making these connections is still another crucial ingredient of the "new" world history. It emphasizes connectedness and interactions of all kinds—cultural, economic, political, religious, and social—involving peoples, places, and processes.

It makes comparisons and finds similarities. Emphasizing both the comparisons and interactions is critical to developing a global framework that can deepen and broaden historical understanding, whether the focus is on a specific country or region or on the whole world.

The rise of the new world history as a discipline comes at an opportune time. The interest in world history in schools and among the general public is vast. We travel to one another's nations, converse and work with people around the world, and are changed by global events. War and peace affect populations worldwide as do economic conditions and the state of our environment, communications, and health and medicine. The New Oxford World History presents local histories in a global context and gives an overview of world events seen through the eyes of ordinary people. This combination of the local and the global further defines the new world history. Understanding the workings of global and local conditions in the past gives us tools for examining our own world and for envisioning the interconnected future that is in the making.

Bonnie G. Smith
Anand Yang

The Balkans
in World History

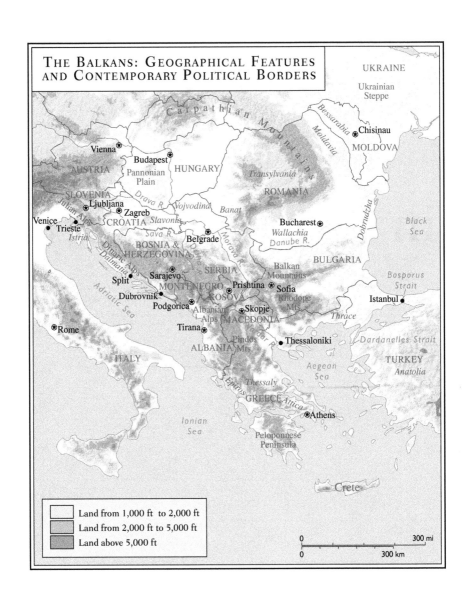

THE BALKANS: GEOGRAPHICAL FEATURES
AND CONTEMPORARY POLITICAL BORDERS

UKRAINE

Ukrainian
Steppe

Carpathian Mountains

Bessarabia

Moldavia

Chisinau

MOLDOVA

Vienna

Budapest

AUSTRIA
Pannonian
Plain

HUNGARY

Transylvania

ROMANIA

SLOVENIA

Julian Alps

Ljubljana

Drava R.

Vojvodina

Banat

Zagreb

Slavonia

Dobrudcha

Venice

CROATIA

Sava R.

Trieste

Istria

BOSNIA &
HERZEGOVINA

Dinaric Alps

Dalmatia

Belgrade

Morava R.

Bucharest

Wallachia

Danube R.

Black
Sea

BULGARIA

Balkan
Mountains

Bosporus
Strait

Split

Sarajevo

SERBIA

MONTENEGRO

Prishtina

Sofia

Dubrovnik

Adriatic Sea

Podgorica

KOSOVA

Albanian
Alps

Rhodope
Mts.

Istanbul

Skopje

MACEDONIA

Thrace

Dardanelles Strait

Rome

Tirana

Vardar R.

Thessaloniki

ITALY

ALBANIA

Pindos
Mts.

Aegean
Sea

TURKEY

Anatolia

Epiros

Thessaly

GREECE

Attica

Ionian
Sea

Athens

Peloponnese
Peninsula

Crete

Land from 1,000 ft to 2,000 ft

Land from 2,000 ft to 5,000 ft

Land above 5,000 ft

0   300 mi

0   300 km

The Balkans as Borderland and Melting Pot

In the historical and literary imagination, the Balkans loom large as a frightening but ill-defined space. Most attempts at classification focus on geography (the Balkan Mountains give the area its conventional name) or, from the mid–nineteenth century, on the set of prejudices attached to the term by local and outside observers. Historians have generally been less concerned with defining this region in positive terms and taking as a starting point the cultural, historical, and social threads that make it a coherent, complex whole.

The Balkans is a borderland where four of the world's great civilizations overlapped to produce a dynamic, sometimes combustible, multi-layered local civilization. Here the cultures of ancient Greece and Rome, Byzantium, Ottoman Turkey, and Roman Catholic Europe met, clashed, and sometimes merged—a land that no single culture was ever able to dominate completely. The resulting cultural layering, as it appears in Bosnia, perhaps the quintessential Balkan space, is captured beautifully in Ivo Andrić's novel *A Bosnian Chronicle*. Not coincidentally, the narrator of this passage is a foreigner; for the local inhabitants, Balkan cultural profusion was so commonplace as to be unremarkable.

> When you make your way through the bazaar, stop by the Yeni mosque. There is a high wall round the whole grounds. Inside, under huge trees, there are some graves. No one knows any longer whose they are. The people know that once, before the arrival of the Turks, this mosque was the Church of St. Catherine. . . . And if you look a little more closely at the stone in that ancient wall, you will see that it comes from Roman ruins and tombstones. And on a stone built into the wall of that mosque you can clearly read the steady, regular Roman letters of a fragmented inscription: "Marco Flavio . . . optimo. . . ." And deep beneath that, in the invisible foundations, lie large blocks of red granite, the remains of a far older cult, a former temple of the god Mithras.

On one level, then, the history of the Balkans is found in the succession of civilizations that have conquered the region.

Such layering of civilizations, however, is not the only way in which the region displays a mixed or hybrid character, nor is it unique. Successive civilizations have left their traces in many areas of the world, although perhaps in a manner less apparent to the naked eye than here. More unusual is that this layering has been complemented by the extraordinary variety found in the area at any particular time. A description of guests at a caravan stop in Bosnia sometime in the eighteenth century in a short story by Andrić illustrates this aspect of Balkan life:

> Sulaga Dizdar with three tax collectors traveling on business; two Franciscan friars from Kreševo who were going to Istanbul regarding some kind of lawsuit; an Orthodox monk; three Venetians from Sarajevo with a young and beautiful woman. It was said that they were ambassadors from Venice traveling overland to the Porte—they were carrying a letter from the Pasha in Sarajevo and were accompanied by a bodyguard, but they held themselves aloof and looked dignified and suspicious. There was a trader from Serbia with his son, a tall quiet youth with a sickly red face.

Variety of this sort remained characteristic of Balkan life into the twentieth century. This, for example, is how the Nobel Prize–winning writer Elias Canetti remembered his birthplace in the years just before World War I:

> If I say that Rushchuk is in Bulgaria, then I am giving an inadequate picture of it. For people of the most varied backgrounds lived there, on any one day you could hear seven or eight languages. Aside from the Bulgarians, who often came from the countryside, there were many Turks, who lived in their own neighborhood, and next to it was the neighborhood of the Sephardim, the Spanish Jews—our neighborhood. There were Greeks, Albanians, Armenians, Gypsies. From the opposite side of the Danube came Rumanians. . . . There were also Russians here and there.

Precisely this kind of ethnic and linguistic mixing was what French chefs had in mind when they decided to borrow a Balkan geographical name (Macedonia) to describe a mixed fruit salad—"macédoine des fruits."

The Balkans, then, have been characterized by exceptional variety, particularly compared to their neighbors in Western Europe, where more homogeneous states formed by the early modern period. In great measure, Balkan heterogeneity was created, sustained, and amplified because of another crucial feature: the Balkans, through most of recorded history, has been a land in between. The border separating the eastern and western halves of the Roman Empire lay athwart the Balkan Peninsula. Rome would collapse as a political power by the fifth century CE, but it remained the ecclesiastical center of Western Christianity, and the border between Byzantine Christianity (Orthodoxy) and Roman Catholicism would roughly correspond to the ancient line of demarcation between the empire's halves. After the fall of the Byzantines in 1453, the line of separation between the Muslim Ottoman Empire and Christian Western Europe would cut across the Balkans, as would, in the twentieth century, the southern divide between communist Eastern Europe and the West.

This more or less permanent border state meant that the Balkan region was to be influenced but never fully controlled nor peopled by the larger civilizations that lay outside it. Although these civilizations tended to control the region at whatever external borders they were able to establish, within these borders, the local inhabitants were generally left to themselves. Over time the populations frequently intermingled, and local life was indelibly altered by some of what the outsiders brought. Creative reworkings by local people of outside influences led to the creation of hybrids that modified the civilizations of their conquerors to fit local conditions. These modifications left permanent impressions on almost every level of life: day-to-day customs, language, literary and artistic traditions, patterns of trade and economy, and politics and religion.

When the Greeks colonized the coasts along the Southern Adriatic and Black Seas between the eighth and fourth centuries BCE, they made little effort to penetrate the hinterlands, but their trading networks ensured that the barbarian tribes—as the Greeks understood them—who lived there would be exposed to Hellenic civilization. Later, the Romans built roads and fortified cities throughout the Balkans, but they were never sufficiently numerous to displace the native populations who lived outside urban areas or in the inaccessible mountain ranges so characteristic of the region's geography. With the migrations of Slavic tribes into the region in the sixth to eighth centuries CE and the arrival of Turkic Bulgars at approximately the same time, the ethnic and linguistic mosaic of the region changed again. These newcomers settled down in the more fertile areas, in time becoming the most numerous population of the region, and their pagan traditions were melded first with Byzantine and Roman Catholic culture, then strongly influenced by Ottoman Turkish civilization.

In various locations in the Balkans, the mixtures of foreign civilizations produced different results, depending to some extent on the length of time local inhabitants were exposed to a given outside influence. Thus, the lands that became Hungary were for the most part beyond the geographical reach of Hellenic civilization. Byzantine Greek influences were also weaker there than in the lands to the south and east. Nevertheless, because these were Roman provinces, they were brought within the orbit of classical pre-Christian civilizations, traces of which survive today. The Catholic Church eventually succeeded in converting the Hungarians, but these lands would be in Ottoman hands for most of the sixteenth and much of the seventeenth century. Conversely, modern Western European influences were muted in European Turkey until the nineteenth century, while those of Byzantine and Ottoman culture were paramount. Even these poles, however, were never fully insulated from each other, as the sack of the Byzantine capital Constantinople by European Crusaders and the intensive interactions between Byzantines and Hungarians in the eleventh and twelfth centuries attest. Overall, then, the Balkan region can be divided into a core—the area in which all of these influences interacted most intensively—and a periphery, in which a single influence came to be relatively dominant. The core Balkan regions are today's Albania, northern Greece, Macedonia, Bulgaria, Serbia, Bosnia and Herzegovina, southern Romania, and parts of Croatia. The periphery includes southern Greece, Turkey, much of the Adriatic coastline (Dalmatia, Montenegro, and Albania), northern Romania, and southern Hungary.

Geographically, the Balkan Peninsula presents a paradox, for it is simultaneously accessible and inaccessible. The most obvious features on a topographic map are mountains. Though they do not rise as high as the Alps to the north and west (the highest peak in the Balkans, Rila in Bulgaria, is a bit under 3,000 meters), they cover some 70 percent of the region. As is true of other mountainous regions (the Caucasus most notably), the barriers to movement caused by the difficult terrain encouraged the formation of microcultures. They also made it difficult for outside invaders to control the entire area. This remained as true in the twentieth century, when the Nazis tried unsuccessfully to wipe out guerrilla bands in Greece and Yugoslavia, as it had been in the fifteenth, when the powerful Ottoman armies spent twenty fruitless years trying to subdue the Albanian rebel Skanderbeg.

Yet the mountains of the Balkans do not provide a complete barrier to invasion. The peninsula can be penetrated through a number of mountain passes, as well as along its eastern flank, which is open to the Romanian and Ukrainian lowlands and from there to the steppe that stretches from the northern shores of the Black Sea to Mongolia.

The majority of invaders used this route to enter the Balkans, from the Celts in the fifth century BCE to the Magyars (Hungarians) in the tenth century CE. The Balkans are also open to penetration across the Dardanelles and the Bosporus, the narrow straits separating the peninsula from Asia Minor. It was by this route that the first farmers arrived some eight thousand years ago from the more advanced civilizations of the Middle East. This was also the route of the Ottomans, who would be the overlords of the peninsula from the fifteenth to the nineteenth century.

Successive invaders tended to occupy the flatter and more fertile areas along the floodplains of the rivers that run through the Balkans, pushing earlier settlers into the less desirable mountain regions. These rivers, the Danube most notably in the north, but also the Drava and Sava in the northwest, the Drina and the Morava in the center, and the Vardar to the south, provided natural highways through at least part of the area, which was also accessible along its long coastline on the Adriatic, Ionian, Aegean, and Black Seas. Although much of the Balkan Peninsula was forested at the end of the last ice age (approximately 10,000 BCE), little of that remains today. The coastal lands, characterized by a temperate Mediterranean climate, had been denuded by the Middle Ages, and native vegetation was replaced by imported crops such as wine grapes, figs, and olives. The interior plains, where the climate is harsher and generally drier, were gradually brought under cultivation from Neolithic times, although wars and invasions frequently depopulated the peninsula, encouraging the reemergence of vast forests that existed into the modern era. The mountains themselves, the realm of those who had been forced out of the fertile lowlands, became centers of herding, for the climate was too harsh and the soil too poor for most crops. They also provided a haven for outlaw bands, whose exploits would be celebrated throughout the region and who provided significant assistance to national independence movements in the nineteenth century.

The mixture of peoples in the region was encouraged not merely by Balkan geography but also by the character of the Ottoman Empire, which, like the Roman and Byzantine empires that had preceded it, was explicitly multiethnic and multicultural. While West European states underwent a slow but steady process of homogenization, beginning in the fifteenth century, gradually imposing on their citizens a single linguistic, legal, social, political, and cultural system and often killing or expelling those unwilling to accept it (as happened in Spain to the Muslims and Jews), the Ottomans offered their subjects a high degree of autonomy in their day-to-day affairs. They made no effort to impose the Turkish language, did not actively force conversion to Islam, and allowed legal disputes not involving Muslims to be adjudicated by local leaders. At the same time, Ottoman control allowed for and sometimes even encouraged the mobility of various groups within the borders of the empire.

When, in the seventeenth and eighteenth centuries, the Austrian Habsburgs seized the northern parts of the peninsula from the Ottomans, they, too, encouraged mixing of peoples. The Habsburgs settled colonists from the north on lands that had been depopulated by war and the flight of Turkish settlers, and they encouraged Serb migrants from the south to live in and protect the so-called military frontier (*Krajina*) between the empires. In short, rather than creating the conditions for a European-style homogenization of the region, Ottoman and Habsburg rule allowed for the continuation and even intensification of a state of affairs in which the mix of peoples and traditions could be perpetuated into the modern age.

Various groups of inhabitants in the Balkans did, however, recognize differences among themselves. Given their wide variety of linguistic, religious, and cultural practices and their physical proximity, they could hardly have failed to notice such differences. Already in the Middle Ages a number of the Balkan peoples had created distinctive civilizations and were competing for territory and influence. But medieval Balkan states were built on the principle of loyalty to a monarch and his family rather than to a culturally defined national group, and they never demanded that foreigners on their territory assimilate to their way of life. The Ottomans divided the citizens of their empire not by nationality but by religion, an organizing principle that slowed the development of national consciousness among local populations. And even if local populations did not necessarily like each other or their Ottoman overlords, their differences did not prevent the various peoples of the Balkans from living together in relative peace. Traces of these long-term, intensive interactions can still be seen in unrelated Balkan languages, for example, that came to share not only many words but also grammatical features. Anthropologists have noted shared traditions as well, such as a rainmaking ritual in which a young woman covered in a costume of leaves would sing and dance through the village: this ritual was practiced among Greek, Albanian, Romanian, and Slavic speakers throughout the region, and it is not clear who borrowed it from whom. Studies of the northern districts of Albania, Kosovo, and Montenegro indicate that the traditional clothing of this region displayed Muslim, Christian, and even Jewish symbols, regardless of the wearer's religion.

The Balkan Peninsula developed its diverse civilization over many centuries as geographic factors, combined with the inability of any one civilization to assert complete control over the local populations, encouraged variety. These factors were all in place by 1700, so the Balkans, as a region and a culture, can be said to have already existed by this time. However, it was not yet *the Balkans*, the stereotype developed during the past 150 years or so: a warren of small and spiteful peoples, states, and would-be states racked by racial and ethnic hatred always ready to burst into violent conflict, a region whose spirit, in the words of the German Count Hermann Keyserling, is that of "eternal strife."

The Balkan Peninsula did not become *the Balkans* until locally born but European-educated elites made attempts to superimpose Western European ideas of nation and nation-state—ideas that had grown up more or less organically in Western Europe over hundreds of years—onto the existing mix of peoples in the region. This process got underway as Ottoman control over the peninsula gradually weakened, which created a power vacuum that was filled first by local Muslim warlords and then, gradually and more permanently, by local Western-European-educated Christian men backed covertly or overtly by the Western European great powers (England, France, Austria, Russia, Prussia). For these men, the natural cultural and political unit was not the heterogeneous and multilingual Balkan mosaic but the nation, imagined as a historically continuous, ethnically pure group defined by a shared language, culture, and, usually, religion. They believed that such a unit, once it had achieved consciousness of itself as a national group, should aspire to an independent political existence in a state built by it and for it, a state that, ideally, would contain all the members of a given nation and no one else. Not coincidentally, such a state would also give the cultural, political, and economic elites who brought it into being a privileged position.

But as a result of geography and history, nations of this sort did not exist in the Balkans, so the European-educated elites had to create them, through a cultural process of national "awakening." Drawing on dim memories of medieval states and claiming exclusive ownership of linguistic and cultural practices that were often shared with many other Balkan groups, these elites first forged a national consciousness among their fellows, then attempted to create politically independent states. But the reality of Balkan mixing meant that each newly constituted Balkan state found that large numbers of potential members of its nation lived outside its borders, and every state contained numerous inhabitants who did not belong to the majority.

The political history of the Balkans in the nineteenth and twentieth centuries was the working out of the contradiction between the reality that had been created by the logic of Byzantine and Ottoman traditions and the new reality that Western European ideologies of the nation-state introduced. Despite some efforts to create a synthesis between the two—a Balkan "third way"—this contradiction proved irreconcilable. Balkan heterogeneity proved incompatible with the formation of the kinds of modern nations and states that Europeans and European-influenced Balkan elites saw as natural and normal. Thus, the Balkans became *the Balkans* when the diversity that had traditionally characterized the region went from being a fact of life to a problem that could only be solved through violent separation.

The conflicts that characterized relations between states in this region throughout much of the modern period, then, can be understood primarily as attempts to synchronize the borders of the nation and the state, eliminating heterogeneity in the name of national consolidation. Because none of the national groups was strong enough to achieve this goal on its own, each tended to call for help from outside powers, who had reasons of their own for keeping the Balkan pot boiling and acted to exacerbate rather than alleviate tensions. For large numbers of people, the results were disastrous. Among those who suffered were groups who lived in small and scattered populations throughout the region, including Jews, Roma (also called Gypsies), and Vlachs (nomadic shepherds whose language descended from Latin).

During the twentieth century, the Balkan states gradually lost their traditional characteristics. Massacres, population exchanges, border changes, and the assimilating power of national educational systems began to erase cultural differences among the peoples. In addition, the selective destruction of cultural monuments (particularly those associated with Muslim culture), the expurgation of "foreign" words from national languages, and the wholesale adoption of Western European lifestyles and habits made the heritage and history of the region less apparent. Finally, in the wake of changes in the world's geopolitical boundaries after World War II and then again after the collapse of communism, the region lost its borderland quality. Greece became an essentially monoethnic state by the 1920s and was firmly part of the West after World War II. Albania, Romania, and Bulgaria lost most of their "Balkan" characteristics by the 1950s.

Only Yugoslavia remained typically "Balkan," containing a multiethnic population and striving to create a balance between Western capitalism and Soviet communism. The collapse of Yugoslavia and the creation of more or less ethnically pure successor states in the 1990s [*last of the part of the Balkans*] brought the history of *the Balkans* to a close. The phrase is still used to describe a stereotypical vision of the region (and *balkanization* is used to refer to hostile breakups in other parts of the world), but what this phrase evokes no longer has much connection with the reality of the Balkan Peninsula. A few small islands of traditional Balkan diversity remain in Macedonia and Bosnia and Herzegovina, but the region as a whole is rapidly being integrated into Western Europe, and a new borderland is being created to its south (Turkey) and its east (Moldova, Ukraine, Russia). For the first time since the days of the Romans, the Balkan Peninsula is fully under the control of a single civilization. *The Balkans* is being transformed, for better or worse, into Southeast Europe.

CHAPTER I

Beginnings: From Prehistory to the Byzantine Empire

For a modern observer in the Balkans, traces of the region's prehistory and early history are readily found. Visitors can explore the tells (sites of ancient settlements where successive layers of homes created large artificial hills) of the Bulgarian plains, the Lion Gate at the fortress of Mycenae in Greece, or the magnificent remains of Diocletian's palace in Split, Croatia. Other traces can be heard in the Greek, Albanian, and Romanian languages whose progenitors were all spoken on the Balkan Peninsula in classical times. Still others can be tasted, in the olives and wine grapes brought to the Balkans by prehistoric settlers more than four thousand years ago. Even some of the modern political problems of the Balkans can be linked directly to classical times—such as the ongoing dispute between Greece and the Republic of Macedonia as to which state has the right to claim the legacy of Alexander the Great.

Evidence of human habitation in the Balkans dates back almost fifty thousand years, and anatomically modern humans appeared here, as elsewhere in southern Europe, somewhat more than thirty-five thousand years ago, during the Upper Paleolithic period. These early humans lived, as the archeological record reveals, in small and mobile groups, hunting, exploiting the bounty of lakes and seas, gathering wild plants, and fashioning stone tools. Patterns of life on the Balkan Peninsula were similar to those elsewhere on the continent at this time, though populations appear to have been sparser, for although the region was for the most part spared the glaciation that accompanied the last Ice Age in Europe (which ended around 10,000 BCE), it lacked the populations of large mammals that roamed the northern parts of the continent and could support larger hunting groups.

Around the time of the Mesolithic period (approximately 10,000 BCE to approximately 7000 BCE in the Balkans), hunter-gatherer groups began to settle into somewhat more permanent habitations. On terraces cut into the banks of the Danube River between today's Serbia and Romania, at a site called Lepenski Vir, archeologists have discovered remarkably well-preserved foundations of early shelters. The oldest, dating from around 7000 BCE, incorporate both wood and stone and were probably covered with skins. Although the builders did not yet make pottery, nor did they have domesticated crops, the care and effort taken in the building process indicate that they already possessed an appreciation of place and sufficient organizational and technological skills to alter their landscape in a conscious way. These same people also had the desire and leisure to create sculptural works, both abstract and anthropomorphic, which are presumed to have had ritual significance of some kind.

A true revolution came to the Balkans in the period between 7000 and 6500 BCE (the beginning of the Neolithic period). Three crucial innovations have been documented at sites scattered widely over the region: sustained cultivation of the land (excavations have revealed traces of domesticated wheat, barley, peas, and beans); fired clay pottery for storage, cooking, and ceremonial use; and new domesticated animals, particularly goats and sheep, which joined animals domesticated somewhat earlier, including cattle and pigs. Despite these innovations, tools

Most of the houses found at Lepenski Vir in Serbia contained stone sculptures, including the heads of humans, deer, and fish. The figures of humans tended to have fishlike mouths and to emphasize such features as eyes and eyebrows, becoming more exaggerated and less realistic over time. Erich Lessing/Art Resource, NY.

continued to be fashioned of flaked stone, and the newly agricultural societies continued to hunt, fish, and gather the forest bounty that had earlier been their sole source of subsistence. Given the sparse population of the region in the Mesolithic period and the fact that these innovations first appeared in the southern Balkans and spread toward the north, it seems likely that the original farmers consisted not of indigenous peoples but rather of colonists who arrived from the Middle East through Asia Minor, where these same processes had been initiated perhaps a millennium earlier. Indigenous populations did not necessarily disappear completely, but the evidence suggests they were for the most part absorbed by newcomers.

Balkan outsiders at the time

Little is known about the interactions of the Neolithic peoples of the Balkans either within their own communities or across communities. It is clear that in the period from about 6000 to 4000 BCE, the Neolithic inhabitants tended to build and rebuild their communities on a single site. The remains of these sites, called tells, can still be seen today as raised mounds formed by the successive layering of simple wood and mud huts. The largest, such as Karanovo in Bulgaria, are almost forty feet tall and show evidence of more or less continuous habitation for some two thousand years. Built on open sites near floodplains where the most fertile soils lie, they lack fortifications, an indication that organized warfare was not yet a problem. Presumably, populations were still relatively sparse and there was enough room for all.

Increasing technological change also occurred during the Neolithic period. Evidence from excavations indicates that pottery was first produced in small quantities and used for limited ceremonial purposes (the remains of burnt incense have been found in some pots, for example). But later in this period, specialized potters began to work, a sign that a division of labor had been woven into the fabric of life; pots are more abundant, they are better and more consistently made, and they are used for a broader variety of purposes, including cooking. The incised or painted designs employed on pottery were highly consistent within specific geographic areas, implying that groups of people in the Neolithic landscape cultivated particular patterns that served to set them off from neighboring groups. In addition to creating pottery for storage and cooking, Neolithic peoples also produced many clay figurines in the shape of animals and humans. It is likely that these had ritual significance, but we will never know the precise role these objects played in their spiritual world.

Neolithic pottery

Pottery was not the only material used to create objects for purposes of ritual and decoration. By around 5000 BCE in what is today Bulgaria, local populations had developed techniques for the mining and smelting of copper and gold. They had not yet invented the technology needed to create harder alloys such as bronze, however, so the objects they made were not sufficiently sturdy to replace stone in tools and weapons. Rather these items, including rings, earrings, and pendants, appear to have been primarily ornamental or ritualistic in character.

For reasons that remain unclear, traumatic changes occurred throughout much of the Balkan region around 4000 BCE. Long-inhabited sites were abandoned, ornamental work in clay and metal appears more rarely, and there are signs of a general depopulation. Although some grand explanations for this phenomenon have been proposed—including the theory that peaceful, female-led indigenous peoples suffered invasion at the hands of war-like, male-dominated Indo-European tribes (carriers of the ancestral language for all but a handful of the modern European languages)—no hard evidence can be found to substantiate them.

Whatever the reasons for this relative dark age, however, a recovery began in around 3500 to 3000 BCE, by which time significant alterations had occurred in the lives of the peoples inhabiting the Balkan Peninsula, particularly its southern portions. These changes were spurred by the introduction of new crops, new technologies, and perhaps new peoples as well that arrived most probably from Anatolia. The man-made landscape, at least in the coastal regions, began to take its modern form with the introduction of such crops as the olive and the grape. Olive oil and wine have since formed mainstays of the diet along the coasts of the peninsula. Technologies applicable to war—such as the creation of metal alloys for use in weapons—also arrived at approximately this time.

Settlements were no longer constructed on open floodplains but rather in more defensible hilltop positions, an indication that warfare had become endemic. In the northern Balkans, adjacent to the Black Sea, there appeared steppe peoples from the east, whose domestication of the horse and the ox gave them a new degree of mobility. Doubtless, societies became more stratified as they became more complex, and it is reasonable to suppose that hierarchies of power were in the process of being institutionalized. Certainly, in somewhat later periods, we find evidence that warrior groups had come to take a dominant position. Members of the warrior elite were buried together with their weapons in individual graves quite differently from the way nonwarriors were treated. Though the graves usually hold males, graves of female warriors have also been found.

Few traces of these societies remained apparent in later periods, however. The technologies they developed would continue to be refined and employed, and the crops and domestic animals they introduced remain crucial to the Balkan economies and cuisines to this day. But later inhabitants of the peninsula lost all memory of their distant ancestors, whose presence in the landscape could be sensed only in the raised tells and the occasional grave site that farmers undoubtedly turned up. It was not until the early twentieth century that archeologists began to make systematic attempts to recover what had been an almost completely forgotten chapter in Balkan prehistory.

After about 2000 BCE, we move from the age of prehistory to that of history, at least in the southernmost parts of the peninsula. Although a great deal would later be forgotten or distorted, the deeds and lives of at least some members of the oldest literate Balkan civilizations (Mycenaean on the peninsula itself and, even earlier, Minoan on the islands of Crete and Thira) remained in the collective memory. They can be found in the Greek stories of the Minotaur, the lost city of Atlantis, and the Trojan War and in sites such as the Lion Gate at Mycenae (completed around 1250 BC). Still, as is the case for the Neolithic period, the bulk of our knowledge of early Balkan civilizations has come through modern archeological research, which has provided a wealth of detail about ancient material and spiritual life, often corroborating events and practices that had been described in myths and legends.

The first inkling of the extent of Minoan civilization came through excavations conducted by Sir Arthur Evans in Knossos on the island of Crete at the beginning of the twentieth century. We still know little about the Minoans or the internal organization of their civilization, but the massive remains of stone cities and the tablets inscribed with the so-called Linear A script (as yet undeciphered) indicate that this was a sophisticated and literate society. By the middle Minoan period (approximately 2200 BC to 1700 BC), Knossos was an enormous labyrinthine structure, with imposing formal rooms, extensive storage depots, and indoor plumbing. Population estimates for Knossos range from fifteen to fifty thousand people, whose lives were bound up with an economy based not only on agriculture but also on specialized crafts and long-distance trade that linked the Cretans with Egypt in the south, Phoenicia in the east, and mainland Greece in the north. Minoan craftsmen were highly skilled, both in the creation of monumental structures and luxury goods such as carved ivories, vases, and wall paintings, including spectacular frescoes that depict young men and women leaping over the horns of bulls, an activity that may have had ritual significance and is undoubtedly related to the story of the Cretan Minotaur.

The first civilization in the Balkan Peninsula itself about which we know a fair amount was that of Mycenae. At their height, in the thirteenth century BCE, the Mycenaeans controlled much of today's Greece, especially along the coastal regions as well as the islands. The remains of Mycenaean roads, dams, and bridges, their distinctive tholos (beehive-shaped) tombs, and the enormous stone blocks of their palace walls (built sufficiently well to have stood for more than three thousand years) indicate that the Mycenaean rulers were able to command large numbers of workers and skilled engineers. Their craftsmen excelled in finer work as well, producing spectacular golden objects, high-quality bronze weapons and tools, carved figures in ivory, and elegant pottery vessels. The Mycenaens were also explorers, who sailed along the coasts of the Aegean Sea and also through the Bosporus to the western shores of the Black Sea. Mycenaean civilization ended relatively suddenly and violently in around 1200 BC, though the cause of the destruction remains unclear.

The classical Greeks, whose civilization began to take form in the eighth century BCE, surmised that the Mycenaeans were their distant ancestors. They identified the colossal ruins of their cities with the dwelling places of legendary heroes—Achilles, Agamemnon, Odysseus—who had lived in the days when gods still walked the earth, had used bronze weapons and tools as opposed to the more modern iron ones, and who must have had supernatural help to build their monumental palaces. But because the classical Greeks could not read the Mycenaeans' Linear B alphabet and because, despite their enquiring cast of mind, they did not have any interest in archaeology, there was no direct investigation of the earlier civilization. Little was known about the Mycenaeans until the German archeologist Heinrich Schliemann, attempting to prove that Homer's stories in *The Iliad* and *The Odyssey* were factually based, began to dig at Mycenae in the mid-1870s. Schliemann was convinced that the golden objects he discovered at Mycenae dated from the time of the Homeric heroes. Later archeologists, however, have demonstrated that these objects predate the period described in *The Iliad*. They were also able to show, by deciphering the Mycenaean alphabet, that these people had used a version of Greek, proving that Mycenaean civilization was indeed an antecedent to that of the classical Greeks of the eighth to fourth centuries BCE.

Classical Greek civilization flourished in Attica and the Peloponnesus and reached its peak with the cultural and political achievements of Athens in the fifth century BCE. Building on earlier traditions, including those of the Balkan Peninsula (Mycenae) as well as Crete, North Africa

(Egypt), and the Near East, the Greeks created a civilization that forms the backbone of practically all of later Western culture. As opposed to the relatively large and centralized states of the Minoans and Mycenaeans, classical Greece was divided into small city-states that sometimes banded together in alliances and at times fought destructive civil wars. For much of the classical period, the most powerful and influential city-state was Athens, and it is simply impossible for us to imagine a world without the legacy of Athenian civilization: the philosophical questions posed by Socrates, Plato, and Aristotle; the Greek myths and Homeric epics recorded at this time; the tragedies of the playwrights Aeschylus, Sophocles, and Euripides; the comedies of Aristophanes; the architectural and sculptural monuments of the Acropolis; the statecraft and rhetoric of Athenian democracy; and the historical writing of Thucydides and Herodotus. The peripatetic Herodotus left the most extensive extant descriptions of the "barbarian" peoples who lived to the north, that is, in the Balkans proper. These peoples had presumably continued to live during the height of Mycenaean civilization as they had for millennia. For although the Mycenaeans explored the coasts, they did not penetrate into the Balkan Peninsula beyond their base in mainland Greece. Rather, the important influences on the Balkans north of Greece in this period came primarily from the steppes to the east and from the metalworking cultures of the Carpathians and Transylvania to the north. These Balkan cultures borrowed metallurgical technologies developed in today's Germany along with weapons and fighting techniques derived from the steppe peoples. The bronze weapons that have been found in warrior graves indicate the skill and beauty of the work of the Carpathian masters. Finds of similar objects from today's Romania and Serbia show that in this period (around 2000 to 1500 BCE), the influence of this culture had spread well into the northern Balkans.

The classical Greeks, unlike the Mycenaeans, founded permanent colonies along the western shores of the Black Sea and began to come into extensive contact with the inhabitants of the Balkan interior. By the mid–seventh century BCE, there were Greek settlements on the Aegean coast of Thrace and along the western shores of the Black Sea as far as the mouth of the Danube. These were primarily trading depots where Greek luxury goods were exchanged for grain and slaves, but they had a significant cultural and economic influence on the peoples of the interior of the eastern Balkans and Black Sea steppes, whose economy came to be at least partially dependent on trade with the Greeks. Already by the seventh century BCE, some inhabitants of the Black Sea steppes were apparently engaged in commercial agriculture, supplying grain to

Athens in exchange for Greek-produced luxury goods. In his *History* (written in the mid–fifth century BCE), Herodotus described the various tribes that lived in and around the Balkans, and it is from his descriptions that almost all of our "eyewitness" knowledge of these illiterate peoples derives. His primary interests were the Scythians, the catchall name the Greeks gave to the nomadic and seminomadic inhabitants of the steppes to the north of the Black Sea and to the Thracians, whose territory stretched from the Aegean Sea in today's northern Greece to the Black Sea coast of today's Bulgaria. Herodotus also provided colorful accounts of the customs of the Thracian tribes that lived immediately to the north and east of the classical Greek city-states.

> The Thracians who live above the Crestonaeans observe the following customs. Each man among them has several wives; and no sooner does a man die than a sharp contest ensues among the wives upon the question which of them all the husband loved most tenderly; the friends of each eagerly plead on her behalf, and she to whom the honour is adjudged, after receiving the praises both of men and women, is slain over the grave by the hand of her next of kin, and then buried with her husband. The others are sorely grieved, for nothing is considered such a disgrace.
>
> The Thracians who do not belong to these tribes have the customs which follow. They sell their children to traders. On their maidens they keep no watch, but leave them altogether free, while on the conduct of their wives they keep a most strict watch. Brides are purchased of their parents for large sums of money. Tattooing among them marks noble birth, and the want of it low birth. To be idle is accounted the most honourable thing, and to be a tiller of the ground the most dishonourable. To live by war and plunder is of all things the most glorious.[1]

The Thracians remained an independent group on the fringes of Greek civilization throughout the classical period, which ended after the disastrous civil wars of the late fifth and early fourth century BCE. The Thracians would be fully Hellenized by the Macedonians, whose rise to prominence began in 360 BCE when Philip became king after his older brother was killed in battle with the Illyrians, who bordered Macedonia on the north. Philip transformed Macedonia from a provincial kingdom on the fringes of the classical Greek world to its undisputed leader. As opposed to the city-states of the classical period, Macedonia was a centralized state under a king who was the political, religious, and military leader. Indeed, when he was assassinated in 336 BC, King Philip was presiding over a marriage ceremony at which his own statue was to be paraded along with that of the twelve major

Greek gods. Until recently, little was known about the achievements of Macedonian civilization, which was always considered derivative of classical Greece. Excavations in the 1970s near the town of Vergina in Greek Macedonia, however, yielded spectacular finds, including a royal tomb identified as having belonged to Philip himself. These excavations indicate that far from semibarbarian warriors, the Macedonians were fitting heirs to their Greek forebears, producing colorful frescoes and spectacular golden objects.

Macedonia's significance in the region increased during the short but glorious reign of Philip's son Alexander, whose first achievements included victorious campaigns in the Balkans, which his armies traversed all the way to the Danube. Control of the Balkans, however, was of little importance to Alexander, who focused on dreams of conquering Asia. By 334 BCE, he was ready to set off on the string of campaigns that would earn him the name Alexander the Great and whose ultimate result would be to spread Hellenistic civilization over much of the Near East. After Alexander's death in 323 BC, his kingdom disintegrated, and Macedonia proper lost its central position in Greece, particularly after its territories were plundered by marauding Celts in the early third century BCE.

In addition to memories of their military exploits, the Macedonians also bequeathed to the Balkans a territorial dispute that continues to this day. The Macedonians in Philip and Alexander's time clearly spoke Greek. However, it is not clear whether the original Macedonians were Greek by origin. More likely, they represented an amalgamation of some other group with the Greek colonists who had moved to the area in early classical times. From the nineteenth century, however, Greek politicians would use the Greek-Macedonian historical connection to justify Greek claims to the entire territory that could be called Macedonia, including lands that today lie in Bulgaria and the Republic of Macedonia. When it became independent in 1991, the Republic of Macedonia attempted to create its own connection with the glorious Macedonian past, using the rising sun that was the symbol of ancient Macedonia as its national emblem. The ensuing diplomatic spat saw Greece blocking the use of Macedonia as the name for this fledgling country, insisting that it be called FYROM (Former Yugoslav Republic of Macedonia) in official international contexts; the dispute continues to this day.

The Celts were not the only group to take advantage of the power vacuum that followed the weakening of the Macedonian kingdom after Alexander's death. Perhaps the most important were the Illyrians. Unlike the Thracians, the Illyrians, though defeated by Philip and Alexander, were never assimilated into Greek civilization. They continued to live to the north of Macedonia, in what is today Albania, as well as perhaps Dalmatia and Bosnia. As with the Macedonians, the Illyrians have left a controversial legacy in the Balkans. Those ancient writers who discussed the Illyrians did not differentiate among the various tribes who lived in the region they called Illyria, and as a result, it is impossible to know whether all the people described as "Illyrian" in classical sources were in fact related to each other and if so how. Where they once lived would be immaterial were it not for the fact that twentieth-century Albanian historians have attempted to prove a direct line of descent between the Illyrians and today's Albanians. If true, this would make the Albanians, along with the Greeks, the oldest of the indigenous Balkan peoples to survive to the present day, and, more important, it could allow today's Albanians to stake historic claims to areas of the Balkans where, in the modern period, Albanian presence has been limited. Given the frequency with which historical claims to territory have been used for the purposes of expansion in the region, such assertions are potentially explosive. Not surprisingly, historians and archeologists from neighboring countries remain skeptical of Albanian claims, conceding that while some Illyrians were probably ancestors of today's Albanians, this cannot be said for all the peoples who were once called Illyrians.

In any case, there was unquestionably an Illyrian kingdom centered near Lake Shkodër in today's Albania in the third and second centuries BCE. Like many other tribal-based groups that inhabited territories adjacent to those of richer and more stable Balkan societies, the Illyrians lived from a combination of subsistence agriculture and piracy. They were a constant thorn in the side of the Macedonians as well as the state of Epiros in western Greece, but they also served as allies and mercenaries for those kingdoms when the price was right. The Illyrians also caused problems for the expanding Roman Republic, which became the leading power in the region by the second half of the third century BCE.

According to the Greek historian Polybius, in around 230 BCE the Roman Senate sent emissaries to Queen Teuta, the Illyrian leader, to force her to rein in Illyrian pirates who were attacking Roman shipping in the southern Adriatic.

Audience having been granted them, they began to speak of the outrages committed against them. Teuta, during the whole interview, listened to them in a most arrogant and overbearing manner, and when they had finished speaking, she said she would see to it that

Rome suffered no public wrong from Illyria, but that, as for private wrongs, it was contrary to the custom of the Illyrian kings to hinder their subjects from winning booty from the sea. The younger of the ambassadors was very indignant at these words of hers, and spoke out with a frankness most proper indeed, but highly inopportune: "O, Teuta," he said, "the Romans have an admirable custom, which is to punish publicly the doers of private wrongs and publicly come to the help of the wronged. Be sure that we will try, God willing, by might and main and right soon, to force thee to mend the custom toward the Illyrians of their kings." Giving way to her temper like a woman and heedless of the consequences, she took this frankness ill, and was so enraged at the speech that, defying the law of nations, when the ambassadors were leaving in their ship, she sent emissaries to assassinate the one who had been so bold of speech. On the news reaching Rome, the woman's outrage created great indignation and they at once set themselves to prepare for an expedition, enrolling legions and getting a fleet together.[2]

The Romans and Illyrians would skirmish many times during the succeeding decades, before Rome achieved final victory over the Illyrians in 167 BCE. As was customary, the Romans divided the booty of the conquest (said to have included 27 pounds of gold and 19 of silver as well as 220 Illyrian pirate vessels) among their soldiers, allies, and the treasury. Still, for at least the next 150 years, tribes the Romans called Illyrians continued to live a semi-independent existence in the Dalmatian and Herzegovinian mountains. Even after their final incorporation into the Roman Empire, their name lived on in the Roman province of Illyricum, a name that would be revived by Napoleon when he conquered the region in 1809.

As opposed to the Greeks, who confined their settlements to the coasts, the Romans colonized the coast and the interior of the Balkans. As a result, their presence was felt almost everywhere on the peninsula and remains visible today. Among the cities they founded or enormously expanded were Emona (Ljubljana), Singidunum (Belgrade), Serdica (Sofia), Philipopolis (Plovdiv), Salonae (Solin, near today's Split), and Dyrrhachium (Durrës). Roman remains, some in an excellent state of preservation, can be seen in these and many other parts of the Balkans, providing contemporary inhabitants of the region with a clear visual link to the Roman past. The greatest Roman engineering feat in the region was the construction of the 520-mile-long Via Egnatia, the first major road they built outside the Italian peninsula, which linked Dyrrhachium in today's Albania with Byzantium (Istanbul), later to become the capital of the Eastern Roman Empire. Along with a more northerly route that followed river valleys from Emona through Singidunum, Serdica, Philipopolis, and Adrianople (Edirne), these roads have remained the main lines of land communication through the Balkans. In the early twenty-first century, a European Union project to connect Istanbul to the Albanian coast by modern highway along the route of the old Egnatian Way serves as a testament to the wisdom of Roman engineers.

Although most of the region would lose its Roman character in the wake of the barbarian invasions that began in the fourth century CE and culminated with arrival of the Slavs in the sixth and seventh centuries, some coastal cities of the Adriatic (Dubrovnik, Split, Zadar) would still contain Latin-speaking populations for hundreds of years. Curiously, the Roman presence lasted longest in what had been a marginal part of the empire: the Dacian provinces, which after Emperor Trajan's victory over the Dacians in 106 CE became Rome's farthest-flung territory to the northeast. The Romans killed off the local nobility, exiled or

The Roman amphitheater at Pula, in present-day Croatia, dates from the first century CE. *It could hold some 25,000 spectators and is the best preserved Roman amphitheater in the world.* Cameraphoto Arte, Venice/Art Resource, NY.

enslaved much of the native population, and encouraged colonization of the province by settlers from other parts of the empire. Although barbarian invasions forced the Romans to pull back to the Danube some 150 years later, the colonists, who presumably mingled in time with the remaining Dacian population, stayed behind to become the ancestors of today's Romanians as well as, perhaps, the ancestors of the Vlachs, nomadic herders who speak a Latin dialect and can still be found sprinkled throughout the Balkans.

Although the Balkan Peninsula was never a central focus of Roman policy, some key events of the early Imperial period took place there. It was along the Egnatian Way that the armies of Julius Caesar and Pompei maneuvered in 48 BCE, before fighting their decisive engagement in Thessaly. The battle of Philippi, fought between Caesar's heirs Octavian and Marc Antony and his assassin Brutus also took place in the Balkans. Emperor Diocletian, whose economic, military, and administrative reforms at the end of the third century CE transformed the empire, was born in Illyria, and it was to Illyria that he retired in 305. (Under Diocletian the empire was divided into a western and eastern half, with most of the Balkans in the latter.) In Split he built himself an enormous palace that is still in use today, an amazing example of the ways in which local populations have continued to employ the traditions and objects left to them by the Romans.

Also born in the Balkans was the Emperor Constantine, though his rise to power began in Britain. In a series of military campaigns beginning with the Battle at Milvian Bridge near Rome (312 CE) and culminating with his victory at Chrysopolis in Asia Minor (324 CE), Constantine reunited the empire. In the course of these campaigns, he also became a Christian, though there is much evidence that his Christianity was rather unorthodox, mixing the still not fully formed doctrines of the Church with a pagan cult devoted to the sun god. Nevertheless, he supported the Church and donated enormous sums for its expansion. It was as a Christian that Constantine took up residence in his newly founded capital Constantinople, which was formally dedicated in 330 CE. Built on the site of an older Greek settlement called Byzantion (which had been colonized as early as the mid–seventh century BCE), the city is located in a supremely strategic position athwart the land and sea routes connecting Europe and Asia.

Constantine's decision to locate the seat of his power in this city was to have a momentous impact on the Roman world. It signified a turning away from the West, from Latin and pagan Rome (which rapidly declined into political insignificance after barbarians sacked it repeatedly in the fifth century) and toward the Greek and Christian East. The city itself expanded rapidly and soon outgrew the walls Constantine had laid out. Under the Emperor Theodosius in the early fifth century, massive walls were constructed to protect the city from attacks from the north. They would serve their purpose for more than one thousand years. By the reign of Emperor Justinian, which began in 527, Constantinople was the largest city in Europe, with a population approaching half a million. It was at this period that many of the most recognizable early Byzantine monuments were built, including the Church of Holy Wisdom (Hagia Sophia) and the underground cistern meant to allow for the storage of sufficient water to see the city through a long siege.

Hagia Sophia, constructed in the sixth century CE, *is most notable for its enormous dome. As described by the contemporary historian Procopius, it was "distinguished by indescribable beauty, excelling both in its size, and in the harmony of its measures. . . . The church is singularly full of light and sunshine; you would declare that the place is not lighted by the sun from without, but that the rays are produced within itself." After the conquest of Constantinople in 1453, the church was turned into a mosque and the minarets were added. The basic design of Hagia Sophia was adopted for all the major Ottoman-era mosques of Istanbul. In 1935, the mosque was deconsecrated and turned into a museum. Library of Congress, LC-DIG-ppmsca-03864.*

The civilization centered in Constantinople was a curious amalgam of old and new, as seen in the names that have been used to describe it. The empire is conventionally called the Byzantine, but its inhabitants never used the term, calling themselves instead Rhomaioi (Romans) and considering themselves the heirs of the moribund Western city of Rome. They were, however, thoroughly Hellenized heirs, down to their use of Greek, which replaced Latin as the main language of the empire by the mid–sixth century. Though the empire would suffer ups and downs, including times when practically all of its territories were lost and it appeared that the capital itself was certain to be destroyed, it managed to retain its integrity until the imperial city was captured by West European crusaders in 1204. After this catastrophe, the empire was able to rebound, though never fully recover, before its final destruction by the Ottomans in 1453.

The empire's strength derived from its unique blend of secular and religious institutional power. It was first and foremost a Christian state, whose basic doctrines were defined by the church fathers, the church councils, and the decisions of the various Byzantine emperors. Although during the early centuries, the church was racked by heresies and doctrinal disagreements, after the final victory of those in favor of icon worship in 843, the doctrine of the Eastern Orthodox Church was essentially fixed. By comparison with Catholicism (and later Protestantism), Orthodoxy was a static religion, which placed great stock in liturgy and ritual and tended to be less concerned with individual achievements. In the Byzantine scheme of things, the emperor, chosen by God, was more powerful than any Western ruler. It was the emperor, not the patriarch (the title given to the spiritual leader of each of several national branches of the Orthodox church), who presided over church councils and expounded dogmatic pronouncements. This was true even before Christianity became the state religion (which occurred around 380), for Constantine himself summoned and presided over the first church council at Nicaea in 325. Although Catholic popes could make even the most powerful Catholic kings bend to their will at times, the Byzantine patriarch was appointed by the emperor and could be dismissed by him. When one eleventh-century patriarch tried to challenge this arrangement, he was arrested, beaten, and thrown into prison, where he died before a trial could occur.

Although much did change and evolve in Byzantine society in the course of its millennium-long existence, one of the great illusions propounded by this civilization was that change was unnecessary and even impossible. Harmony, order, precedent, symmetry, and stasis were

THE BALKANS IN THE 7TH–8TH CENTURIES

Moravians

East Slav Tribes

KINGDOM OF THE FRANKS

Danube R.

AVAR KHANATE

LOMBARD KINGDOM

Pannonian Slavs

Slovenes

Aquileia

Ravenna

BULGARIAN KHANATE

Black Sea

Sirmium (Sremska Mitrovica)

Danube R.

Pliska

Salonae (Split)

Ragusa (Dubrovnik)

Serbs

Serdica (Sofia)

Mesembria (Nesebar)

Philippopolis (Plovdiv)

Adrianopolis (Edirne)

Constantinople

Dyrrhachium (Dürres)

Thessalonicae (Thessaloniki)

LOMBARD KINGDOM

Adriatic Sea

BYZANTINE

EMPIRE

Aegean Sea

Smyrna (Izmir)

Ephesus

Ionian Sea

Athenae (Athens)

Byzantine Empire
Kingdom of the Franks
Avar Khanate
Bulgarian Khanate
Lombard Kingdom
Slav settlement in Byzantine territory

0   300 mi
0   300 km

supreme values, as can be appreciated in the classic lines of a building like Hagia Sophia, the beautifully preserved mosaics in Ravenna, the incantatory melodies of Byzantine church music, or the following words of advice, given to the emperor by an eleventh-century courtier:

> You are straight, true, stiff . . . steadfast, firmly fixed, lofty . . . an impartial judge, unwavering in judgment . . . a secure counselor, noble,

unshaken in [stormy] waves. . . . Where is there anger in you, where are there streams of laughter, where are there traces of rage, and where is there the babbling of speech? Where is there boasting, or violence, and a wily mind? Where [is there] a knitting of the brows or an angry expression? For there are no unseemly qualities in you, neither easily excited emotion . . . nor delight, nor any graces, nor much laughter.[3]

Order was preserved not merely by a complex series of secular and religious rituals, but also through the efforts of a large bureaucracy. A Byzantine handbook outlining imperial protocol from the end of the ninth century describes the positions and roles of more than five hundred officials who were to attend formal receptions in the palace. If one adds the administrative personnel in provincial cities, thousands of people must have been on the imperial payroll. These men were generally highly educated, both in theology and in the Greek classics. Indeed, much of the legacy of classical Greece was preserved through the Byzantine educational system. Imperial bureaucrats frequently vied for power with the empire's military leaders, who were based primarily in outlying territories, where they had extensive civil and military control. At the height of Byzantine power, from the ninth to the eleventh centuries, their relations were generally harmonious, but in later periods local lords began to assert control of the territories under their jurisdiction, leading to a gradual weakening of the empire. Both bureaucrats and military men were supported by the labor of farmers, who made up the bulk of the population.

Although little is known about agricultural practices in the Byzantine Empire, they had apparently changed little from the classical period (the only surviving Byzantine agricultural treatise, from the sixth century, is a reworking of a classical prototype). Farmers worked primarily on their own small plots, producing sufficient food to support their families and to pay a variety of taxes. A considerable number of peasants worked on land belonging to monasteries, the state, or the emperor himself, and in later periods many worked on the extensive estates of provincial lords. In the cities, craft industries were regulated by guilds, including organizations for butchers, fishmongers, bakers, and producers of silk goods, jewelry, and perfumes. Not surprisingly in such an orderly state, prices were strictly controlled.

In the early Byzantine period, the empire directly controlled the bulk of the Balkan Peninsula. And even though a good portion of the region would be lost during various ebbs of Byzantine power, the Imperial City and its culture nevertheless exerted a crucial influence on developments in the Balkans between the seventh century, when the Slavic and Bulgar invasions destroyed almost all vestiges of Roman urban life in the central and northern Balkans, and the thirteenth century, by which time all of the Slavic invaders had converted to Christianity, many to the Orthodox ritual of the Greeks.

CHAPTER 2

The Medieval Balkans

From the sixth century until the beginning of the Ottoman conquest of the Balkans in the latter half of the fourteenth century, the final "permanent residents" of the Balkan Peninsula migrated to the region. These were the Slavs—most important because eventually most numerous—but also the Turks (first Bulgars, a small warrior elite that led a group of Slavs into the Balkans in the sixth century, and then Ottomans) in the south and east, Magyars (Hungarians) in the north, and finally the Roma (Gypsies), who would eventually spread over the entire peninsula. These peoples joined those already present in the region—the Greeks, the Illyrians (likely ancestors of the Albanians), and the Romanized Dacians (ancestors of the Romanians and, probably, the Vlachs). Although there would be a great deal of mixing among these peoples over the centuries as well as many conflicts between them, the ancestors of all the modern Balkan nations were thus present by the end of the medieval period.

Though they had arrived as a motley array of loosely organized tribes, the Balkan peoples developed new forms of political organization between the eighth and thirteenth centuries, largely under the influence of Byzantine models. At some point during this period, the Bosnians, Bulgarians, Croats, Hungarians, Romanians, Serbs, and Slovenes would develop independent, though generally fragile, states. All would lose their political independence for some five hundred years after the Ottoman conquest, but hazy memories of medieval glory, preserved in religious institutions, architectural monuments, and oral peasant culture, would remain, later to be marshaled by nineteenth-century intellectuals and politicians for nation-building projects. Competing claims to territory based on the borders of these medieval states continue to bedevil the region.

Finally, the medieval period saw the Christianization of the majority of the Balkan peoples. Although many inhabitants of the Balkans had probably been Christians in the fifth century, after the Slavic invasions of the sixth and seventh centuries, the peninsula again became pagan, with the exception of Constantinople, Salonika, and the walled cities on the Adriatic coast. In the course of the next three hundred years, missionaries from Constantinople or from Rome would evangelize the newcomers. Competition for influence in the region between the two main Christian centers was fierce, and ultimately it was split, approximately along the line of division between the former eastern and western halves of the Roman Empire. The northern and western Balkans became primarily Catholic, while the southern and eastern Balkans became primarily Orthodox. Conversion to Christianity, initially by political leaders and later by the common folk, brought enormous changes, for Christianity of whatever branch permeated the daily life of all the Balkan peoples (though never entirely destroying the vestiges of pagan traditions). Rituals connected with saints' days, festivals, and church holidays and intimate events such as baptisms, marriages, and funerals all took on a Christian coloration. Furthermore, Christianity brought literacy, at least to the elites, which opened new possibilities for cultural development. The architectural and artistic monuments of Christianity produced in this period, including the magnificent frescoed churches on the shores of Lake Ohrid in Macedonia and the equally magnificent monastery churches in Kosovo, can still be found throughout the Balkans.

In their heyday, the Romans controlled the entire Balkan Peninsula. And though the Balkan provinces were never of central concern to Rome, they were crisscrossed by imperial highways and dotted with significant urban centers, along the coasts and inland. By the sixth century, however, weakened by waves of invasions, the eastern half of the Roman Empire controlled the peninsula only as far north as the Danube River. Beginning in the middle of that century, raids across the Danube by peoples the Romans had never before encountered became endemic; and by the mid– to late seventh century, Slavs, who apparently made up the bulk of these invaders, had replaced Byzantine forces and settled practically the entire Balkan Peninsula. Byzantine settlements remained only along the coasts and in the lands immediately surrounding Constantinople. Greek remained the main language in the southernmost portions of the Balkans, but Slavic settlements were scattered even there, reaching as far south as the Peloponnesus.

Although the Byzantines called them by a single name, the Slavic invaders entered Byzantine territory in an uncoordinated manner under the command of individual warlords and without any centralized political structure. It is not entirely clear how the Slavs managed, in the course of a century and a half, to occupy almost the entire Balkan Peninsula. Although there is evidence that in earlier centuries they had been peaceable, by the sixth century they had become bellicose, as the following account by the historian John of Ephesus (written in about 585) indicates:

> The accursed people the Slavs arose and passed through the whole of the Hellades, through Thessaly and Thrace, conquering many towns and forts, wasted and burnt, looted. They overcame the country and settled it freely without fear as if it were their own, and strange to say to the present day inhabit it and sit secure in the lands of the Romans without fear or cares, plundering, murdering, and burning.[1]

He seems particularly surprised that the Slavs remained, and this was indeed something new in the Byzantine experience. Previous invaders had been nomads on horseback who attacked swiftly and then withdrew, but the Slavs had come to stay. Having exhausted the available plunder, they settled down and began to farm, using simple wooden and then iron plows to cultivate grains, vegetables, and fruits, herding flocks of domestic animals, brewing beer and making wine. And yet, it is difficult to imagine that there could have been enough Slavs north of the Danube at the beginning of their invasions to populate the entire region. Presumably, the Slavs assimilated many of the local inhabitants, especially in the more fertile areas where their farming settlements were congregated (indigenous populations remained in the less fertile mountainous areas, however). The fact that the Slavs quickly adopted techniques in metalworking and architecture that had been typical of earlier settlers in the region is one strong indication that they mixed with and absorbed the local populations rather than killing or expelling them.

The victorious Slavs reintroduced paganism over the territory they controlled. Because pagan practices were vigorously suppressed after the Slavs themselves were Christianized in later centuries, little is known about the religious traditions of these then-illiterate peoples, but it appears that the Slavs had a well-developed set of beliefs concerning the world of evil spirits (some of which survived in rural areas into the early twentieth century). Demons could inhabit any place, from the home to the fields and forests to the streams, and they had to be placated. The dead were particularly dangerous, including those who became vampires, male blood-sucking spirits whose name is apparently of Balkan origin. Festivals took place at strategic points of the year, in particular midsummer's eve. The tradition of lighting a bonfire on this night and dancing and singing around it, still practiced in some places today, derives from this pagan festival. The most important divine figure was thought to control lightning, rain, and by extension, fertility. We also know that the early Slavs cremated their dead, for no skeletons from this period have been found in or near their early settlements.

Compared with the rich material culture of late antiquity, that of the early Slavs seems poor. Archaeologists have recovered large quantities of hand-made pottery, some with incised decorations, but the invaders do not appear to have used potter's wheels. By the ninth century, however, the Slavs had developed a professional pottery industry, with wheel-made objects fired in closed kilns at relatively high temperatures. Early Slavs were skilled smiths as well and produced a wide variety of iron implements, from knives to plowshares. Precious metals were rare, but small amounts of gold and silver made their way from Constantinople into Slav territories even at this early period. The Bulgar warrior aristocracy was fond of wealthy display, and a few beautiful gold objects made in the region have been found.

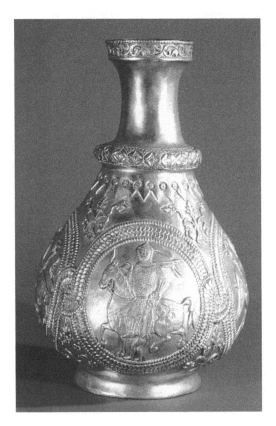

This finely crafted gold jug, made in Bulgaria in the ninth century, depicts a mounted and well-armored Bulgar warrior dragging a hapless captive by the hair. National Museum of History, Sofia, Bulgaria.

The inventory of objects used by the early Slavs was not, however, as limited as the archeological evidence suggests. For where Balkan dwellers in late antiquity had used ceramics and metals intensively, the Slavs employed cloth, skins, and wood, which are far more perishable. Nevertheless, some later pictorial and written descriptions of daily life do exist, and their accuracy has in part been confirmed by recent finds of preserved objects buried deep in bogs in more northerly regions inhabited by Slavs. Men wore a knee-length, long-sleeved tunic fastened at the waist by a leather belt. Underneath, they wore tight breeches and leather shoes or boots. Women wore linen or woolen dresses of variable fashion. We can guess from traditions that appear to have been passed down for many generations that unmarried women wore their hair loose, but married women donned some kind of headdress, which could be quite elaborate. Earrings, rings, and bracelets of silver and semiprecious stones frequently found in graves attest to a love of adornment.

After they settled down, the Slavs constructed settlements. Their dwellings were usually sunken-floored, one-story huts; in one corner was either a stone or clay oven, used for both heating and cooking. The main structure was often flanked by smaller outbuildings. Such settlements were not built to last. Nearby fields would be intensively cultivated for some years, then abandoned as the land became gradually less productive, for the early Slavs do not appear to have practiced crop rotation or fertilization to prolong the life of their fields. They did not have to develop such techniques because the abundance of available land in these sparsely populated areas meant they could simply move a short distance away, clear new land by hacking away larger trees and burning the remaining brush, and rebuild their simple homes. This settlement pattern helps to explain their relatively quick spread throughout the region.

Life in the Roman Balkans had been focused on cities, but the Slavs lacked experience with urban living. The invaders, led by a chief and his military retinue, plundered whatever territory they could and then settled down to a life of subsistence farming supplemented by occasional raids. Having been looted repeatedly, the majority of the Balkan towns were abandoned in the course of the seventh and eighth centuries, with urban life reduced to Constantinople and Salonika in the south and the coastal cities of Ragusa (Dubrovnik), Spalato (Split), Trogir, and Zadar along the coast. From this time on, a relative paucity of cities, especially in the core Balkan region, would remain a feature of life until the twentieth century. The economy also contracted. Although archeologists have unearthed coins from the fifth and sixth centuries CE throughout the Balkans, almost no Byzantine coinage from the seventh and eighth centuries has been found here, suggesting that people relied on subsistence farming and barter and that long-distance overland trade had all but disappeared.

By the ninth century, however, the Byzantine Empire, which had almost collapsed in the two previous centuries, was again expanding. Enterprising merchants ventured out on the old Roman roads. Sea traffic, though harried by piracy, revived along the Adriatic and Black Sea coasts. Under the influence of the Byzantines, the once-marauding Slavs and Bulgars began to form centralized kingdoms and to rebuild urban areas, generally around the courts of local princes. These included Pliska and Preslav in Bulgaria as early as the ninth century and Ras in Serbia in the eleventh. New cities stimulated trade in the Balkan interior, which slowly revitalized, despite the almost constant warfare characteristic of this period. By the twelfth century, mining was revived and expanded, particularly in Serbia and in Bosnia, as the names of newly founded towns such as Srebrenica and Olovo (Silvertown and Leadtown, respectively) attest. To develop mines, rulers encouraged skilled foreign laborers, such as German-speaking Saxons, to settle on their lands.

Nevertheless, throughout the medieval period and well into the twentieth century, the typical Balkan dweller was a farmer in the countryside. Some were free, others were enserfed peasants, bound to their land. Though detailed contemporary descriptions of Balkan family life do not exist, the basic unit was probably the extended family. We can guess this from linguistic evidence; compared to most other languages, Slavic languages contain an abundance of terms for various blood relatives, necessary to track relationships in complex extended families. Such extended family groupings, sometimes containing more than one hundred relatives in a single household, continued to exist into the twentieth century.

Although the majority of the contemporary Balkan countries trace their ancestry back to medieval predecessors, the states that formed beginning in the ninth century were unlike the later nation-states. Rather than attempting to advance the interests of a people who spoke a common language, shared a religion and customs, and viewed themselves as connected to each other, the medieval Balkan state was primarily the creation of an ambitious ruler who strove to exert control over as large a territory as possible. Rulers generally incorporated local lords in the lands they annexed, regardless of the population of those lands, using either promises—such as continued local autonomy and a share of the booty as the kingdom expanded—or threats of being deposed and replaced by others more loyal. All states were, from a modern perspective, multinational, for they contained speakers of many languages and a variety of cultures. Although the ruling elites in a given medieval state would speak the same language, no Balkan medieval ruler tried to coerce others to accept his customs or language. A 1387 treaty between the Serbian Prince Lazar and the Republic of Dubrovnik explicitly confirmed the existing practice in the region.

> My government has granted them another privilege that they had before. If there should be some dispute between citizens of Dubrovnik and Serbia, let half of the appointed judges be from Dubrovnik and the other half from Serbia, and let it be argued before them, and let the jury for a Dubrovnik person be his own people, Dubrovnik citizens who are from that place or from the nearest location; if both of the contestants desire testimony, let half the witnesses be Dubrovnik people and the other half Serbs; and let none of these witnesses be free to run off. If Saxons should become involved in a dispute with Dubrovnik people, let them be judged as with Serbs.[2]

Balkan kings borrowed the model of a multiethnic state held together by a ruler and his elite from the Byzantine Empire, and it would remain typical for both the Ottoman Empire and later the Austro-Hungarian Empire as well. The diverse character of the state did not necessarily mean that the various groups in a given kingdom liked each other, but they did tolerate each other's presence.

The Byzantine Empire was the model state for most of the medieval kingdoms of the Balkans. Although it had been in crisis when the Slavs and Bulgars arrived, it was, in comparison to the motley group of invading tribes, still a well-ordered bureaucratic state with a functioning royal court, bureaucracy, military, tax-collection system, and centralized religion. Even as they competed with the Byzantines, the Slavs and Bulgars learned from them and ultimately created, in effect, a series of mini-Byzantiums. In imitation of the Byzantine emperor, powerful local rulers attempted in various ways to develop among their subjects a feeling of loyalty to their kingdoms. They built rich capital cities and established elaborate court rituals. They accepted Christianity for themselves and their subjects and encouraged the growth of state churches loyal to the ruler and often dependent on his patronage. The most ambitious kings attempted to develop a network of local lords bound to the state by more than self-interest. A ruler would farm out key territories to his most loyal followers (best of all, his sons), who, while having the freedom to rule their smaller territories as they saw fit, were also to assist the ruler's efforts to expand the state farther. A second step, but one that no medieval Slavic ruler succeeded in taking, would have been to create a bureaucratic caste loyal to the state rather than the sovereign; such a caste formed the backbone of Byzantine power and allowed the empire to survive even periods of turmoil at the top.

The Balkan Slavic kingdoms, however, were prone to fragmentation, and it was rare that such states managed to last more than a hundred years before collapsing after the accession of an incompetent ruler, the rise of stronger neighboring states, or competition from outsiders. The most permanent such competitor was the Byzantine Empire, especially until it fell to the Crusaders in 1204, after which it, too, behaved more like a typical Balkan kingdom than a great empire. In the later medieval period, both the Hungarians in the north and the Venetians along the coasts provided stiff competition for the Balkan kingdoms.

The Bulgars were the first Balkan group to create a state. They had first settled on Byzantine lands in the late seventh century. As they had inhabited territory in close proximity to Constantinople, they were quickly brought into its orbit. As early as 681, the marauding Bulgar chief Isperikh had forced the Byzantines to cede him land south of the Danube, and by the early ninth century, the Bulgars had created a centralized and powerful state. It was at this point ruled by a Turkic aristocracy, which during the next few hundred years became thoroughly Slavicized. Nevertheless, linguists can still trace some fifty words in modern Bulgarian to their origin in the Turkic dialect of the original Bulgars. In the hundred years between the reigns of Khan Krum (803–814) and King Symeon I (893–927), this state expanded from a relatively small territory straddling the Danube to an enormous kingdom that controlled almost the entire Balkan Peninsula.

Symeon, who had been educated in Constantinople, created an ostentatious, Byzantine-style court, which was described by the Byzantine cleric John the Exarch.

> When some poor foreigner from afar approaches the Tsar's city and sees it, he is awed. And when he gets to the gates, when he enters and sees the buildings on both sides, embellished with stones and carved wood, he is amazed. And when he enters the compound and sees the tall roofs and churches, abundantly ornamented with precious stones, inlaid wood and velvets, enters the palace—with its marble and copper, silver and gold—he realizes that he does not know what to compare this to. . . . but if he should happen to see the Tsar inside, sitting, wearing his mantle set with pearls, with the golden necklace about his neck, and bracelets on his arms, girdled with his purple belt with his

sword hanging at his side, flanked by his boyars wearing their golden necklaces, belts and bracelets—well, when he returns home if someone asks "what did you see there," he will answer "I can find no words for it"[3]

Symeon appears to have had aspirations to the imperial crown itself and signed his decrees as the "emperor and autocrat of all the Bulgarians and Greeks." The Byzantines, however, did not succumb to the Bulgarians, and by the late tenth century, they had managed to roll back Bulgarian territorial gains. Though a second Bulgarian empire, centered near Ohrid in present-day Macedonia, temporarily competed with the resurgent Byzantines in the early eleventh century, all the Bulgarian lands were again under Byzantine rule by the middle of that century. Bulgaria would make a comeback in the late twelfth and thirteenth centuries but would never extend as far as it had in the tenth century.

At approximately the same time as Symeon was extending the borders of his kingdom to the south and west, a powerful Croatian kingdom appeared in the northwest of the Balkan Peninsula; whereas the Bulgars looked to the Byzantines, the Croatians, under King Tomislav (ca. 910–928), were more closely connected to the Latin empires of the West. At its height, from the mid–tenth century to the mid–eleventh, Croatia controlled most of today's Bosnia and almost all of today's Croatia with the exception of a few coastal cities that remained under nominal Byzantine sovereignty. As was the case with Bulgaria, however, the kingdom lasted only as long as powerful kings were able to hold it together through force of personality and military power. By 1102, Croatian sovereignty passed to the Magyars (Hungarians), though the Croatians did manage to preserve some of their medieval institutions, particularly their Sabor (parliament) even into the modern era.

The Hungarians were the final group of nomadic invaders to enter and remain in the Balkan lands. Having arrived in the lands that make up today's Hungary by the mid–tenth century, they gradually expanded to the south and west at the expense of both the Bulgarians and the Croatians. Because they were never Slavicized, because the bulk of the territory they now inhabit lies to the north of the Balkans, and because they were firmly in the Catholic rather than the Byzantine orbit, they are not usually considered a Balkan people. Nevertheless, particularly in the period before the Ottoman conquest, Hungarian rulers had extensive territorial interests in the Balkans. By the early twelfth century, the Hungarian kings controlled almost all of today's Croatia (including the major urban centers on the Adriatic coast north of Dubrovnik) and much of Bosnia, in addition to large portions of what is today Slovakia, Transylvania, and Hungary proper.

In the late twelfth century, an important Serbian state began its ascent in the southwest Balkans. Beginning from the humble tribal principality of Zeta (more or less today's Montenegro) in the mountainous hinterland southeast of Dubrovnik, the Serbs expanded rapidly between 1190, when King Stefan I Nemanja extricated the Serbs from Byzantine control, and the mid–fourteenth century, when, under the rule of Stefan Dušan (1331–55), the Serbs controlled enormous territories in what is now southern Serbia, Kosovo, Albania, and mainland Greece. Like Symeon of Bulgaria centuries earlier, Tsar Dušan, as he came to be called, dreamed not merely of a great Serbian kingdom but of inheriting the Byzantine Empire itself. Having moved his capital from Raška (in the southern reaches of today's Serbia) to Skopje, Dušan had the archbishop of Peć crown him emperor of the Serbs, Greeks, Bulgarians, and Albanians. The law code he promulgated in 1349, though clearly derived from earlier Byzantine models, illustrates the high level of sophistication of Serbian feudal society. While it mandates cruel punishments for many offenses (as was typical of the age throughout Europe), Dušan's code covers a wide range of civil and criminal issues, and creates a framework for a well-regulated and hierarchical society. Dušan died before he could attack Constantinople, however, and in the wake of his death, feuding among local lords led to fragmentation and ultimately paved the way for the destruction of the Serbian empire by the Ottoman Turks at the end of the fourteenth century.

Just north of Serbia, in lands contested by both Serbia and Hungary, a series of able rulers created a Bosnian state in the late twelfth century. At its apex, under the rule of Tvrtko I (1353–91), Bosnia was able to take much of the territory of today's Herzegovina from the Serbs, and it controlled the Croatian coastline (except Dubrovnik) from today's Montenegro to just south of Zadar. Though harried by the Hungarians, the Bosnian state retained at least a nominally independent existence until the Ottoman conquest.

In the northern and eastern sections of the Balkans, the principalities of Wallachia and Moldovia struggled to achieve an independent political existence. To the northeast, this area abuts the Ukrainian steppes and the Black Sea coast, and thus was frequently overrun by nomadic tribes until well into the medieval period. Nevertheless, a sufficiently large population continued to speak a Latin dialect (the precursor of today's Romanian), and they eventually succeeded in absorbing the newcomers. Although their independence was precarious, squeezed as they were between the Hungarians to the west, various nomadic invaders to the east, and the Bulgarians to the south, the Orthodox Vlachs, under local leaders called *voivodas,* managed to create states that remained independent until the Ottoman conquest.

When the Slavs overran the Balkan Peninsula in the sixth and seventh centuries, they were unable to capture the principal walled cities along the Adriatic coast. One of these cities, Ragusa (Dubrovnik), founded in the seventh century by Latin-speaking refugees fleeing other coastal areas destroyed by Slav invaders, grew into a small but powerful and exceptionally interesting city-state. While the city's leaders remained mostly Latin and later Italian speakers, Dubrovnik's populace was a mixed group of Slavs and Latins. Inhabitants of a small city-state (the walled city itself probably never had a population greater than 7500), Dubrovnik residents relied on their walls and their wits for survival.

In this fresco painted on the wall of a monastery around 1500, St. Blaise, the patron saint of Dubrovnik, holds the city in his hands. Although the city was almost completely destroyed by an earthquake in the mid-seventeenth century, the basic footprint of the old city remains the same today. Dubrovnik Tourist Board, Dubrovnik, Croatia.

Expert diplomats, they played their more powerful neighbors off one against another, and the city-state managed to remain independent until the early nineteenth century, though acknowledging at various times the sovereignty of the Byzantines, the Hungarians, the Venetians, and the Ottomans. Internally, Dubrovnik was an oligarchy, led for hundreds of years by approximately a hundred noble merchant families.

Dubrovnik exploited its protected site and favorable geographic position as the last major port between the Adriatic and the Mediterranean and as the terminus of land routes from Bosnia and Serbia to the sea to develop into a leading commercial center by the eleventh century. Ragusan merchants traveled far and wide in the Balkans, taking advantage of their republic's independent foreign policy to carve out trading opportunities. In the twelfth and thirteenth centuries, the Ragusans specialized in such products as skins, wool, honey, and salt. By the fourteenth and fifteenth centuries, they were heavily involved in trading the lead and silver mined in Serbia and Bosnia.

Thus, with the exception of the Albanians, the ancestors of each of today's major Balkan populations created an independent state during the medieval period. At their height, the territory of each one of these states was larger than that of its modern successor. As a result, in the modern period each Balkan nation could look back to a time when their ancestors had controlled a great deal of the region. These memories would be revived and exploited by modern-day politicians as historical precedents in favor of a "greater" Bulgaria, Serbia, Croatia, or Greece, often leading to conflict. It is, however, anachronistic to believe that all those who lived in these "greater" medieval states were in fact Serbs, Croats, and so forth. States expanded and contracted, and their populations became, officially at least, subjects of a different overlord. In practice, however, they remained subjects of their local leaders and were probably indifferent as to whether their king was a Serb, a Croat, a Bosnian, or a Bulgarian so long as taxes were not unbearable and their lives and property were secure.

With the exception of Croatia, which at least on paper preserved a modicum of political continuity into the modern era, the medieval Balkan states disappeared completely after the Ottoman invasions of the fourteenth and fifteenth centuries. Other than vaguely preserved memories of bygone glory, little was passed down from the medieval Balkan political experience. What endured and was to leave a permanent imprint both on the physical landscape and on the minds and behavior of most of the inhabitants of the peninsula was the cultural and religious legacy of Christianization.

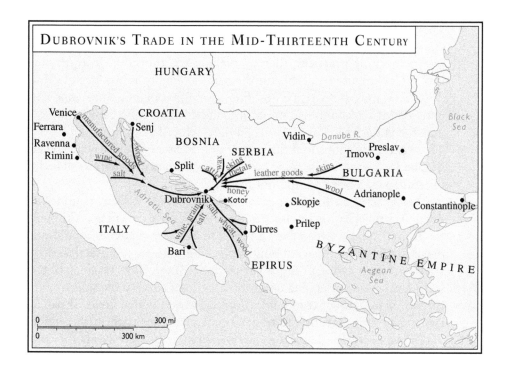

HUNGARY

Venice
Ferrara
Ravenna
Rimini

manufactured goods
wine
salt
wood

CROATIA
Senj

BOSNIA

SERBIA

Vidin
Danube R.

Preslav
Trnovo

Split
cattle
wax
skins
metals
honey

leather goods
skins

BULGARIA

wool
Adrianople

Constantinople

Dubrovnik
Kotor

Skopje

Adriatic Sea

wine, grain
salt
salt, wheat, wood

ITALY

Dürres

Prilep

Bari

EPIRUS

BYZANTINE EMPIRE

Aegean Sea

Black Sea

0   300 mi
0   300 km

Balkan political leaders chose Christianity for a variety of reasons, not necessarily (and sometimes not at all) spiritual ones. As for the common people, we do not know how they reacted to the demand that they change their religion (and with it their entire pagan worldview), but based on analogous cases elsewhere and scanty knowledge from written sources, we can guess that for a relatively long period, pagan rituals and Christian practices coexisted. Indeed, nineteenth-century ethnographers, the first scholars to make systematic studies of the rural Balkan populations, discovered many peasant beliefs and rituals that retained elements of pagan practice (particularly prominent were various defenses against vampires), though they had long been incorporated into a Christian structure.

Christianity had a number of advantages that ensured its eventual triumph over paganism throughout Europe. For one thing, it was well organized. With a strong hierarchy centered in either Constantinople or Rome, it was able to send a coherent and consistent message to the people over a long period of time. Christianity was also supported by local political leaders, who saw it as a unifying force for their kingdoms.

They therefore generally encouraged and supported the work of the clerics. Furthermore, Christianity was flexible in its ability to incorporate preexisting practices, thereby making the transition from paganism to Christianity palatable for the masses. Finally, it produced lasting documentation, both visual and literary. Most obvious were imposing and copiously decorated church buildings, which soon came to dominate the landscape of the few urban areas as well as some rural centers. These churches sponsored the production of literary texts, which, even despite low levels of literacy, provided a permanent tradition that the illiterate pagan priests could not match.

Lying between Rome and Constantinople, the Balkan region was open to evangelization by either of these two Christian centers. Although the formal split between the Eastern and Western churches would not occur until 1054, significant philosophical, doctrinal, and practical divisions had been apparent much earlier. Indeed, the Slav invasions of the sixth and seventh centuries undoubtedly contributed to the split by cutting overland lines of communications between the two great Christian centers. In any case, by the time Christianization began in the eighth and ninth centuries, Latin and Greek Christianity were rivals for converts among the Balkan pagans. In the end, the line of cleavage between the Latin (Roman Catholic) and the Greek (Orthodox) churches would run right through the middle of the peninsula.

This seemingly neat picture, however, masks a complex reality. Indeed, the process of Christianization in the Balkans was really a triangular struggle in which local Slav leaders attempted to achieve as much control over church affairs as possible. In principle, a medieval ruler who accepted Christianity for himself and his state ceded control over religious life either to Rome or Constantinople. However, clever Balkan rulers soon realized that they could exploit their position between the two Christian religious centers. By threatening to go over to whichever branch of the church offered the most autonomy, they pressed for, and often received, important powers usually reserved for Rome or Constantinople, such as the authority to appoint bishops locally and the right to use their own language for the liturgy. They were particularly successful with the Orthodox Church, which was less centrally controlled than the Roman Church—though the danger that Catholics would switch to the Orthodox rite induced the popes to allow greater flexibility in the Balkans than elsewhere in Europe.

The process by which the Bulgarians became Christians illustrates the interplay between the political and religious aspects of conversion in the medieval period. In the early 860s, Khan Boris (who ascended the throne in 852) decided to convert himself and his kingdom, a decision that was probably unavoidable given that the powerful states with whom Bulgaria was competing (the Byzantines, primarily) or with whom it was allied (the Franks) were Christian. Christianity offered a unifying vision that could help bind the state together. The question was from which direction Christianity would come. Initially, Boris sought missionaries not from the nearby Byzantines but rather from his distant allies, the Franks. As they were firmly connected with the Latin Church, these missionaries would have introduced the Roman rite. Given his distance from Rome, Boris probably expected that by accepting nominal papal control, the Bulgarians would be able to achieve significant local independence in church matters, which would have been more difficult to accomplish under the watchful eyes of neighboring Constantinople. The Byzantines, however, were unwilling to allow their close neighbors to go over to Rome, and they dispatched an army to induce Boris to convert to the Orthodox rite. Boris saw the futility of opposing the Byzantine Empire and agreed to be baptized with Emperor Michael III as his sponsor, an event that probably occurred in 864. Simultaneously, he extracted from the Byzantines the official cession to Bulgaria of a small amount of territory, thus ensuring that conversion provided both immediate material as well as long-term spiritual rewards.

But the conversion of the entire population was by no means carried out easily. In 866 a group of still-pagan Turkic Bulgar noblemen revolted. Though Boris suppressed this revolt, which marked the death knell for a separate Turkic presence in Bulgaria, he seems to have been concerned that through the Greek Church the Byzantine Empire was exerting an overly strong influence in his kingdom. To counteract this, Boris made overtures to the pope, who responded by sending missionaries and composing a letter meant to attract Boris to the Latin rite. The following fascinating excerpt was in response to Boris's concern for the salvation of his soul in the wake of his violent suppression of apostasy.

> You described how through divine mercy you received the Christian religion, and how you had all your people baptized, and how after being baptized they revolted with great ferocity against you . . . but through divine power you were ready for them, and you overcame them large and small . . . you cut down with the sword all their leaders and important people, including their offspring, while nothing was done to the lesser and unimportant people. Now you wish to know, with respect to those who were deprived of their lives, whether you committed a sin. But this was certainly not done without sin, since the offspring . . . were slaughtered in their innocence along with the

guilty. . . . But since you have sinned more from zeal for the Christian religion and from ignorance rather than from vice, following your repentance you will receive absolution for these things.[4]

Boris was willing to convert to the Latin rite, but at a stiff price for Rome: he demanded that Bulgaria be given its own archbishop (an important symbol, for it showed that a territory had developed into a major Christian center), and he even suggested a specific candidate. Rome was unwilling to allow a powerful local ruler such latitude. The request languished, and Boris again turned toward Constantinople, where church authorities agreed to give Bulgaria its own archbishop. From this time, the Bulgarian church was firmly part of the Orthodox world, but it developed a high degree of autonomy. Most important, the Orthodox Church did not insist that the Bulgarians pray in Greek but rather accepted the use of the local Slavic dialect for liturgical purposes. This precedent would be followed for other Slavs who converted to Orthodoxy and eventually allowed for a flourishing of literary culture, at first exclusively liturgical but later secular as well, in the local Slavic languages.

It was not merely in the Orthodox world that local rulers were able to carve out a significant degree of ecclesiastical independence. The Croatians, for example, managed to use the in-between position of the Balkans to win from Rome the right to use their own language rather than Latin for the liturgy. Although Rome would make many attempts over the centuries to Latinize the Croatian church, it never completely succeeded.

Both the Bulgars and the Croatians exploited their position between Rome and Constantinople to extract important concessions from their respective spiritual centers. This was the advantage of living in a contested borderland area, and it paved the way for the appearance of a hybrid Christian civilization employing the local languages in the core areas of the Balkans. A comparison of the situation in the core with that in the peripheries reveals the long-term importance of this ecclesiastical competition for later Balkan developments. Although Slavs had overrun a substantial portion of Greece in the seventh and eighth centuries, the Byzantines reconquered the area by the mid–ninth century. Unlike the Slav groups to the north, the Slavs in Greece failed to develop an independent political existence. When Byzantine control was reestablished, many Slavs were forced to move to Anatolia, in accordance with a long-standing Byzantine policy by which populations considered dangerous were transferred to remote parts of the empire. Those who remained adopted the Greek language and customs, and in the course of a century or so became fully Hellenized. Today, only a small number of Slavic place names sprinkled over Greece allows us to appreciate the former extent of Slavic settlement there. The same fate might well have befallen the core areas of the Balkans had not the alliance of powerful local rulers and semi-autonomous church institutions combined to ensure that neither Greek nor Latin would completely triumph.

The most important long-term influence of Christianization was its contribution to literacy among the Slavs. The first alphabet for writing a Slavic language was developed by the missionary brothers Constantine (Cyril) and Methodius for use in distant Moravia, whose ruler Rastislav had requested a bishop and Slav teachers from the Byzantine Emperor Michael III in order to Christianize his kingdom. Although Michael did not send a bishop, he did authorize a mission led by the bilingual brothers, who had been born in the vicinity of Salonika, still primarily a Greek city but with a large Slavic-speaking population. The language into which Cyril and Methodius translated the basic texts necessary for the purposes of evangelical work (presumably the Slavic dialect spoken around Salonika) required only minor modifications in order to be used in Moravia some 750 miles to the northwest. That slight adjustment testifies to the close linguistic relations among the Slavic settlers of the Balkans and Central Europe. This same language, now called Old Church Slavic, also proved sufficiently comprehensible to be used for the evangelization of the Russians, and it remains the liturgical language of Slavic-speaking Orthodox Christians to this day. As none of the Slavic peoples possessed a written language, Cyril devised a suitable alphabet, although not the Cyrillic (which was invented a bit later on the basis of the Greek alphabet) but rather one called the Glagolitic.

The brothers arrived in Moravia in 863 and engaged in their missionary work with the blessing of both the Byzantine emperor and the pope. But by the end of the ninth century, local rulers loyal to Rome suppressed the Slavic ritual in Moravia. The Moravian followers of the Slavic rite fled south and established themselves primarily in Bulgaria, which became the first great center of Slavic literary culture during the reign of Symeon. By this point, the Cyrillic alphabet had been invented, and it replaced Glagolitic in Bulgaria. In parts of the Balkans more distant from Constantinople, however, Glagolitic survived much longer. Indeed, it continued to be used on some isolated Croatian islands into the twentieth century.

Whether in the Glagolitic or Cyrillic alphabet, however, an Old Church Slavic literary culture gradually developed throughout the Balkans during the medieval period. It flourished at the courts of various

This chart compares the Glagolitic alphabet (top line) to the Cyrillic letter corresponding to the same sound (second line). The pronunciation is shown in the Roman alphabet on the third line.

rulers and in the great monastic centers they founded. This was a culture that easily crossed existing political boundaries, spread by itinerant Orthodox monks. Monasticism was a central part of Byzantine and later Balkan Christian life. The first monastery in Constantinople, called Dalmatos, was founded in the late fourth century, and there were some thirty monasteries in the city by the mid–sixth century. As opposed to the Western church, where monks were generally bound to centralized orders such as the Franciscan and Benedictine, Byzantine monastic life was centered in individual monasteries. Those in cities often provided extensive social services, sponsoring hospitals, inns, and schools. Those in the countryside were self-sufficient agricultural communities, in some cases richly supported by noble patrons through gifts of land and serfs. Monks, who had to remain celibate and from whom the higher clergy were exclusively drawn (from the ninth century on), were considered holier and more spiritual than parish priests, who by contrast were required to marry.

Although there were both male and female monasteries in the Byzantine tradition, the greatest center of Orthodox monastic life was the exclusively male Holy Mountain (Mount Athos), a peninsula in northern

Greece that juts out into the Aegean Sea. The first monks came to Athos sometime in the early ninth century, and they lived an ascetic life on this rocky peninsula. By the tenth century, a number of large monasteries had been organized, and Athos became a self-governing community under an elected head with a capital at the monastery Karyes. Although the first Athonite monks spoke Greek, in time other branches of the Orthodox Church, including Georgians, Russians, Serbs, and Bulgarians, founded or took over existing monasteries. Over the years, many Athonite monasteries became quite rich, as patrons gave them the income derived from lands and villagers on the mainland. By the end of the Byzantine period, there were thousands of monks on Athos. Today there are only a few thousand, but they still live according to the ancient monastic laws as a self-regulating community. This monastic community is the only institution to have survived from the Balkan Middle Ages to the present.

Powerful monasteries were also founded throughout the Balkans and were supported by local rulers wishing to display their piety and generosity. When Bulgaria became Christianized, for example, a number of the disciples of Cyril and Methodius, particularly St. Kliment and St. Naum, founded monastic centers. Kliment worked primarily around Lake Ohrid (in today's Macedonia), where he erected some of the beautifully frescoed churches that still dot the lakeshore today (though the impressive paintings were executed a bit later). In Bulgaria proper, John of Rila moved from a monastery near the then-capital Preslav to the inaccessible Rila Mountains in the south to lead the solitary life of a hermit. Other monks followed, however, and by 930 his disciples had founded a monastic house that still exists. The fact that Boris abdicated his throne in 889 to enter monastic life indicates the close relations, typical of Byzantine Christianity, between state and church. His heir, Vladimir, however, attempted to reverse the course of Bulgaria's Christianization. Unwilling to see his life's work undone, Boris emerged from the monastery, deposed and blinded his son (by tradition a blind man could not rule, so this was the standard punishment meted out to political rivals in Byzantium), and passed the throne to his second son, Symeon. Boris then returned to his monastery, where he passed the remainder of his long life, dying in 907.

A similar melding of politics and monasticism took place in Serbia some three hundred years later. In this instance Rastko (1169–1235), the youngest son of the first great Serbian king, Stefan Nemanja, renounced the territory his father wished him to rule and escaped to Mount Athos. Stefan was himself a pious man who had founded a number of monasteries on Serbian territory, including the great center of Studenica. Still, he attempted to force his son, who took the monastic name of Sava, to return to secular life. Sava held firm, however, and his powers of persuasion were such that he convinced his father to retire from the throne and join him on Athos, where the two of them founded Hilander, the Serbian monastery that stands to this day. As was customary, Stefan Nemanja endowed Hilander richly, giving it tenant farmers, the income from a marketplace, two vineyards, four beehives, 3 cattle villages along with their herders and herds, horses, and 30 bushels of salt."[5]

After Stefan's death in 1200, the two sons between whom he had divided the kingdom began to vie for precedence. The elder, Vukan, ruled over the coastal region called Zeta. This area had a large Catholic population, and Vukan himself appears to have converted to Catholicism. With the help of the Catholic Hungarians, he attempted to oust his brother Stefan (his father's favorite and chosen heir) from the central portions of the Serbian kingdom. In the face of this crisis, Sava left Athos in 1207 (though he remained a monk) to rebury his father's body at the monastery of Studenica and to make peace between his brothers. For a decade an uneasy truce prevailed, but Catholicism seemed to be making inroads in Serbia, not surprising given the weakness of the Byzantine church after the sack of Constantinople by the Crusaders in 1204.

The year 1217 proved decisive in settling the border between Eastern and Western Christianity. In that year, Stefan Nemanja's chosen heir accepted a crown from the pope, which signaled a willingness to accept Catholicism as the state religion. Sava, as an Orthodox monk, was opposed to such a move, and to counter it he convinced his brother that the creation of an independent Serbian Orthodox church would be preferable to subordination to Rome. To achieve this goal, Sava traveled to Nicaea, temporarily home of the Byzantine patriarchate. In 1219 an agreement was concluded, and the patriarch ordained Sava as the first archbishop of an autocephalous Serbian church (derived from Greek, *autocephalous* means "having its own head"). Thus, the Serbs achieved religious autonomy from Byzantium but retained Orthodox Christianity in a national church. After the destruction of the Serbian state by the Ottoman Turks, this national church would be the sole Serbian institution to survive.

The legacy of Christianization in the Balkans was not confined to the spiritual realm but extended to artistic culture as well. It is difficult to estimate how much literary work the Balkan Slavs produced in this period because much was undoubtedly destroyed in the invasions and wars that characterized medieval Balkan history. Nevertheless, what remains allows us to see that although most Slavic texts were translations of liturgical works from Greek, some independent literary activity also began in this period. Much of it was in traditional liturgical genres as well, some of the most outstanding being saints' lives of such figures as John of Rila, Stefan Nemanja, and Saint Sava. Writing was also used for secular purposes, however, including law codes, charters, and contracts.

In a few cases, educated men and women produced artistic work of a more personal character; perhaps the most impressive example is Jefimija's "Lament for Baby Uglješa." The daughter of one minor Serbian feudal lord and the wife of another, Jefimija was a well-educated woman who knew both Greek and Serbian. She had the misfortune to live in troubled times. Her life was filled with tragedy, both domestic and historical (the death of her infant son, the death of her husband in battle against the Turks, the destruction of the Serbian state), yet from these tragedies she drew the strength to compose literary works that have made her the first known woman author in the Balkans as well as one of the finest medieval Serbian writers. Her poem, not a formulaic prayer but rather the expression of heartfelt sorrow in the face of an event that was all too common even among the rich and powerful in Byzantine times, was written on the back of a folding icon now located at Hilander on Mount Athos[6]:

> Little icon, but a great gift, bearing the most holy image of the Lord and that of the most pure Mother of God, presented by a holy and great man to my infant son, the princeling Uglješa, who in his innocent and tender years was taken into the eternal family and his body, created in sin, was buried in the grave. Grant, Lord Christ, and You, O pure Mother of God, to me, miserable, that I should see the rising of my soul, as I have seen that of those who bore me and of my little son whom I bore, for whom sorrow burns steadily in my heart, convulsed by the ties of motherhood.

The most visible impact of Christianization, however, was not in literature but in art and architecture. Although at first the artists who built and decorated churches in the Balkans must have been imported from Constantinople, the appearance of hybrid works that blend typical Byzantine styles with local particularities indicate that native artists emerged quickly. One striking example is the haunting icon of St. Theodore, which is made of painted ceramic tiles and depicts a face whose penetrating gaze and haunting expression remain striking for the modern viewer. Another is the monastery church at Gračanica, which starts with a Byzantine floor plan to which it adds an almost baroque series of domes, unlike anything in Constantinople. Fresco painting reached a very high degree of skill and expressive power in this period, as can still be seen in the churches along the shore of Lake Ohrid, as well as in Kosovo, where the walls of Serbian monastery churches are covered in colorful biblical scenes. The artistic and architectural forms inherited from Byzantium and modified in Serbia, Macedonia, Bulgaria, and Romania remained a visible source of inspiration long after the dynasties that created them had crumbled.

An icon of St. Theodore, composed of twenty separate white clay tiles, shows a stylized, full-face image. The emphasis is on the eyes and face, which are clearly outlined and executed with typically strong colors. National Museum of History, Sofia, Bulgaria.

CHAPTER 3

The Balkans under Ottoman Rule

During the millennium-long existence of the Byzantine Empire, many outsiders dreamed of conquering Constantinople and thus simultaneously usurping and inheriting its historical power and significance. These included Balkan rulers such as Tsar Symeon of Bulgaria and Stefan Dušan of Serbia, as well as other invaders such as the Arabs in the seventh century and the Rus in the tenth. Ultimately, none of these groups proved sufficiently well organized to breach the defenses the Byzantines had constructed over the years. Foreigners conquered the city only once, in 1204, when the Catholic Crusaders, egged on by the Venetians, traditional rivals of the Byzantines, decided that the Orthodox Christians were sufficiently heretical (not to mention wealthy) to justify the capture and sack of Byzantium. However, the Catholic Crusaders did not succeed in displacing the Byzantines permanently, and by 1261 the Greeks were back in control of a renewed Orthodox Empire, though one that never regained its economic and military preeminence.

It was not until the middle of the fifteenth century—May 29, 1453, to be exact—that the Byzantine giant, now reduced in power, fell for good to the Ottoman Turks under the command of Sultan Mehmet, "the Conquerer." One theocratic empire then replaced another, and the Muslim Ottomans would rule their multinational empire from Constantinople (which they renamed Istanbul) until the early twentieth century. They controlled much of the Balkan Peninsula for almost as long, leaving an indelible imprint on the Balkan peoples.

The Ottomans came originally from Anatolia, and the capture of Constantinople was not their first Balkan conquest. Their incursions into the Balkans can be likened to a series of tsunamis, with each successive wave breaking farther inland. The Ottomans (whose name derives from a corruption of the name of their first great sultan, Osman) first appeared in the Balkans as mercenaries in 1345, recruited by a high

Byzantine official to help him take the imperial throne. Impressed by the wealth of the decrepit empire, they refused to leave after completing their mission, and by 1354 they had established themselves in Gallipoli, the small peninsula on the European mainland that controls the entrance to the Dardanelles Straits. A wave of attacks from this base put them in control of most of the southern Balkans by the end of the fourteenth century. Nor did they stop after their conquest of the Byzantine capital. The Ottomans continued to expand, until by the mid–sixteenth century, they ruled practically the entire Balkan Peninsula.

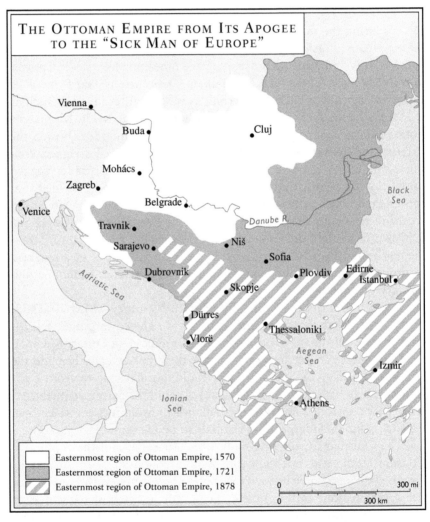

The extent of the Ottoman Empire diminished considerably over three centuries, losing first the area shown in white, then the area in gray, until by 1878 it was reduced to the striped area on this map.

In the late seventeenth and eighteenth centuries, the tide of Ottoman power waned as it had waxed, and they slowly ceded the northern Balkans. For the local populations, however, this meant the substitution of one empire for another, as the Austrian Habsburgs added these territories to their own multiethnic state. The Ottomans continued to weaken in the nineteenth century, as the Habsburgs (rulers of what came to be called Austria-Hungary after 1867) expanded farther into the Balkans, establishing a protectorate over Bosnia and Herzegovina in 1878, and as Greece, Serbia, Montenegro, and Bulgaria became independent states. Nevertheless, the Ottomans did not lose their last footholds in the Balkans until just before World War I.

The Ottoman presence in the Balkans had enormous significance for all of the peoples of the peninsula. In much of the region (Greece, Serbia, Bulgaria, and Bosnia), the Ottoman conquerors destroyed or co-opted the previous ruling aristocracies. They did not, however, eliminate the communities these aristocrats had led. Instead, in exchange for loyalty and regular tax payments, the Ottomans allowed them a broad degree of local control under their religious leaders, thereby guaranteeing the long-term survival of Orthodox communities. The victorious Ottomans also introduced Islam, a religion new to the region, which from this point on competed with Catholicism and Orthodoxy for religious and cultural domination. Islam found large numbers of converts, particularly among the Albanians, Bosnians, and Vlachs, and to a lesser extent among Bulgarians, Montenegrins, and Roma.

Muslim converts as well as Ottoman administrators tended to concentrate in Balkan cities rather than in the countryside, which was dominated, except in Albania and Bosnia, by Christian peasants. As a result, a number of cosmopolitan urban "islands" formed, in which adherents of different faiths and carriers of various cultures lived side by side, learned from each other (albeit grudgingly), and developed what can be called a Balkan civilization. Particularly in such quotidian realms as cuisine, language, and habits of everyday life, this civilization was and remains characterized by an extraordinary interpenetration of influences. Indeed, it would not be an exaggeration to say that precisely the possession of this cultural mix defines being "Balkan" in the local understanding of the word.

Balkan cultural variety was also enriched in this period by the arrival of a large number of Jews, who settled with the encouragement of the Ottomans after having been expelled from Spain in the late fifteenth century. A well-educated people with excellent contacts in Western Europe, they quickly took leading positions in commerce and became an important segment of the urban population. In the rural areas, Ottoman policies encouraged the creation of small individual peasant farms rather than large estates. These land-tenure arrangements eventually played a significant role as the Balkans remained economically underdeveloped in comparison to Western Europe.

There is great historical controversy regarding the legacy of Ottoman rule in the Balkans. The majority of historians from the region describe the Ottoman period in negative terms: Ottoman rule was a "yoke" that stifled development and brought nothing but misery to the Balkan peoples. The view of the Ottomans as semibarbarous occupiers is particularly strong in those modern states with primarily Christian populations that in the nineteenth and early twentieth centuries revolted against Ottoman rule—Greece, Serbia, Bulgaria, and to a lesser extent Romania—thereby bringing down vicious reprisals. Such views resonate with nineteenth-century European propaganda that railed against the "sick man of Europe," as the declining Ottoman Empire came to be called.

Other historians, many from outside the Balkans, disagree. While acknowledging that in the final century and a half of its existence, as the empire declined precipitously and revolts multiplied, conditions for the local populace were far from ideal, they point out that most Balkan inhabitants lived in better material circumstances in the early centuries of Ottoman rule than they had previously. Ottoman control put a stop to the endless local wars (and accompanying misery for the peasant population) that had characterized the late medieval Balkans, and Ottoman taxes were less burdensome than the feudal dues peasants had paid under native rulers (and continued to pay in contemporary Western Europe). The Ottomans were also far more tolerant of differences than were Western Europeans. As a result, if the relatively small medieval Balkan states had to fall under the sway of one of the great empires of the period, they were better off under Muslim rule than they would have been under that of a Western European Catholic empire. After all, the Catholic *reconquista* of Spain in the fifteenth century brought the expulsion of both Muslims and Jews from the Iberian Peninsula, but Ottoman rule in the Balkans led to no such "ethnic cleansing."

There is no question, however, that the initial Ottoman onslaught caused significant change. The first serious Ottoman thrust into the Balkans occurred under Sultan Murad, whose troops captured the city of Adrianople (today's Edirne) as early as 1362. The Bulgarians had submitted to the Ottomans by 1366. Next in line were the Serbs, whose once unified state had collapsed into a number of bickering principalities after Stefan Dušan's death in 1355. A number of Serbian lords banded together unsuccessfully to stop the Turkish advance in 1371. By the mid-1380s, the Turks controlled practically all of Bulgaria and much of today's southern Serbia, having forced the Serbian ruler Lazar to declare his loyalty. Lazar, however, was unwilling to accede to Turkish overlordship, and in 1388 he organized an anti-Ottoman coalition that included Serbs, Bosnians, Bulgarians, Wallachians, and Albanians. They achieved some initial success in the absence of Murad, who was occupied in defending his possessions in Anatolia. In 1389, however, Murad returned and gathered a substantial contingent of Serbian, Bulgarian, and Albanian vassal troops along with his Turkish cavalry. The two armies met on Kosovo Polje (the Field of Blackbirds) on St. Vitus Day (June 28, according to the Gregorian calendar) in 1389.

Although the battle has gone down in Serbian memory as the culminating and crucial national defeat, most contemporary accounts reported it a draw. Lazar was captured and executed after the battle, but Sultan Murad was also killed, apparently by a Serb who tricked his way into his presence. According to later Serbian retellings, this was the hero Miloš Obilić, who went alone to the sultan's camp to prove his fealty after having been slandered by the traitor Vuk Branković, whose disloyalty would lead to the disastrous Serbian defeat. Although there is no hard evidence to support this legend, the importance of treachery in later battle accounts hints at one clear fact: despite the Serbian claim that this was a struggle between Orthodoxy ("the forces of good") and Islam ("the forces of evil"), in reality many Balkan Christians fought on the Ottoman side. Whatever the result of the battle, however, during hundreds of years of Ottoman rule, the Serbs developed in their oral epics a rhetorically powerful tradition of understanding Kosovo as a symbol both of national humiliation and as a hope for future redemption.

The following passage comes from one of these so-called Kosovo songs, as transcribed from an illiterate oral poet in the early nineteenth century by the Serbian linguist and folklorist Vuk Karadžić:

> Flying falcon, grey bird,
> out of the holy place, out of Jerusalem,
> holding a swallow, holding a bird.
> That is no falcon, grey bird,
> that is Elijah, holy one;
> holding no swallow, no bird,
> but writing from the Mother of God
> to the Emperor at Kosovo.
> He drops that writing on his knee,
> it is speaking to the Emperor:

"Lazar, glorious Emperor,
which is the empire of your choice?
Is it the empire of heaven?
Is it the empire of the earth?"

As the poem unfolds, Lazar is told that if he wishes for an earthly kingdom, he need do nothing more than go out and fight the Turks. He will be victorious, but his empire, being of this world, will be brief. If he chooses the empire of heaven, he must "weave a church on Kosovo, build its foundation not with marble stones, / build it with pure silk and with crimson cloth, take the Sacrament, marshal the men, / they shall all die." Lazar's choice of the heavenly kingdom not only "explains" the Serbian loss; it provides a way of seeing the Serbs as a people of God, who choose honor over mere victory, physical suffering over easy glory, and martyrdom over conquest.

The pace of Ottoman conquest did not slow under Murad's successor, Bayezid I. Though his attention was focused on Asia Minor, where he would eventually die in combat with the forces of the Mongol Tamerlane, he nevertheless found the time to make substantial new Balkan conquests and began the process of eliminating the native aristocracy. In 1393 Bayezid's forces captured the last independent section of Bulgaria and pushed north toward the Romanian principalities of Wallachia and Moldavia. Bayezid defeated Prince Mircea of Wallachia in 1395 but left him in place as an Ottoman vassal, counting on Mircea's enmity toward the Catholic Hungarians to keep him bound to the Ottomans. Bayezid also attempted, unsuccessfully, to capture Constantinople. In 1396 he defeated a force of Crusaders under the command of King Sigismund I of Hungary. This left all of central Europe open to the Ottomans, and their advance was checked only by the outbreak of war with Tamerlane in 1402. Although Bayezid's defeat in 1402 might have led to the collapse of Ottoman power, it did not. Tamerlane chose not to follow up his victory by pressing further into Asia Minor but instead turned to China. More important, however, the Ottomans had succeeded in establishing themselves securely in the Balkans, where they regrouped and reorganized.

The early Ottoman state was under the absolute control of the sultan. Indeed, many European observers in the sixteenth century saw the Ottoman Empire as the ideal state for this reason. All major state institutions, including the military, the treasury, and the bureaucracy, were viewed as extensions of the sultan's household. In the first centuries of the empire's existence, between approximately 1300 and 1566, it had the good fortune to be ruled by a series of remarkably talented sultans, who personally led their troops of *ghazis* (warriors of the faith) on an endless series of military campaigns.

The Ottoman Turks themselves were never a large group, however, and the empire's power was not based on their numbers but rather on an exceptionally able bureaucratic and military machine, fiercely loyal to the sultan and chosen on meritocratic principles from various ethnic groups. Here is how the European diplomat Ogier Ghiselin de Busbecq compared the Ottoman state to its European counterparts in the mid–sixteenth century:

> The Sultan himself assigns to all their duties and offices, and in doing so pays no attention to wealth or the empty claims of rank, and takes no account of any influence or popularity which a candidate may possess; he only considers merit and scrutinizes the character, natural ability, and disposition of each. Thus each man is rewarded according to his deserts, and offices are filled by men capable of performing them. In Turkey every man has it in his power to make what he will of the position into which he is born and of his fortune in life. Those who hold the highest posts under the Sultan are very often the sons of shepherds and herdsmen. . . . This is why the Turks succeed in all that they attempt and are a dominating race and daily extend the bounds of their rule. Our method is very different; there is no room for merit, but everything depends on birth.[1]

As far as the military was concerned, in the early years the ghazis were Muslim volunteers who served for the glory of Allah and what plunder they could take, returning to their home villages after each campaign. By the fourteenth century, however, the expanding empire needed a reliable standing army of both cavalry and infantry. The cavalry came to be supported by a feudal principle. Each *sipahi* (as cavalrymen were called) was assigned a sizeable plot of land (called a *timar*) along with the peasants who lived on it. The timar provided sufficient income to outfit and support a man and his horse, and the sipahi were expected to be available for military service at any time and for whatever period necessary. Timars were not hereditary and were held at the pleasure of the sultan, who could reassign them. Thus, if a timar holder refused or was unable to fulfill his duties, his holding would be reassigned to someone more able. Timar holders were not required to be Muslims, and in the Balkans many timars were held by Christians willing to fight for the sultan. Over time, however, many of these Christian cavalrymen converted to Islam.

Timars were farmed by peasants (or *raya* in Ottoman vocabulary), who could be Christian or Muslim and who owned outright the structures on a given parcel as well as agricultural improvements, such as vineyards and orchards. Like the timar holder, however, the peasant did not own the land, which belonged to the sultan. Nevertheless, the raya were considered to hold a permanent and hereditary lease on the land in exchange for the payment of a variety of taxes to the state and the timar holder. In order to function, the timar system required an extremely efficient bureaucracy, whose job it was to ascertain how much land was needed to support a timar holder in a given area and to ensure that timar holders did not demand more in taxes than they were due. Especially in the fifteenth and sixteenth centuries, the Ottoman central authorities went to great lengths to protect the raya from abuses of power by local figures. This system began to break down by the 1590s, however, when central control weakened, and subsequently many timar holders succeeded in laying permanent claim to their lands, which they turned into *chifliks* (estates on which peasant sharecroppers produced agricultural products primarily for export). From this time on, conditions for the raya began to decline. Earlier, in the fifteenth and sixteenth centuries, their circumstances had undoubtedly been better than they had been under medieval Christian rulers and probably also better than in contemporary Western Europe.

Infantry troops came from the janissaries, a corps of slave soldiers. Initially, they were recruited from prisoners of war or were purchased. From the early fifteenth to the early seventeenth century, however, the sultans introduced the practice of *devshirme* (child recruitment), whereby Christian villages were required to provide a periodic levy of young male children. They would be taken to Istanbul, where they were forced to learn Turkish and convert to Islam. Most were taught military skills and became janissaries, forbidden to marry so that they would not be tempted by loyalty to family. The most gifted children, however, were turned over to the palace school in Istanbul. After graduating, they were sent to fill administrative positions throughout the empire. From there, if they had talent and drive, they could rise through the ranks. There is some controversy regarding the feelings of the Balkan peoples toward the devshirme. In many later accounts, it is depicted as a great tragedy, and for some families it must have been. Nevertheless, evidence indicates that some Christian families welcomed the practice, seeing it as a chance for their children to escape the drudgery of peasant life and to make their mark on the world.

Like the rulers of the Byzantine Empire, many of whose traditions they ultimately copied or adapted, the Ottomans placed religion at the center of their worldview. Though they were willing to make use of Christian allies and vassals and generally did not force conversion (at least not on adherents of other monotheistic faiths), the Ottoman state favored Islam over other religions. They were emphatically not racist, however, and upon conversion, a man (only a man, for Ottomans presumed that authority was masculine), whatever his ethnic or racial background, could rise to the highest positions of authority. Men of Christian Balkan origin provided more than half of the grand viziers (the highest administrative office of the empire) in the period from 1453 to 1623, whereas a mere 10 percent of grand viziers were Turkish by birth. Perhaps the most remarkable of these was Mehmet Pasha Sokollu. Born to a Bosnian Christian family in 1505, he was taken to Istanbul as part of the devshirme. Having held a variety of lesser offices, in 1565 he was appointed grand vizier by Suleiman I (the Magnificent). After Suleiman's death, he remained in office under Selim II. Unlike his father, however, Selim II was incompetent. Sokollu, a master administrator, essentially ruled the empire. He led the Ottoman troops in a failed expedition against the Russians in 1569 but retook Tunis from the Holy Roman Empire and reestablished Ottoman rule in the rebellious province of Yemen in 1570. He remained grand vizier until he was assassinated by a political enemy in 1579.

The basis for relations between inhabitants of the Ottoman state of different religions was the *dhimma* (perhaps best translated as "security compact"), according to which adherents of non-Muslim monotheistic religions were afforded the protection of the state in exchange for their willingness to accept the status of second-class citizens. They were required to pay extra taxes and had to submit to a series of humiliating laws that did not apply to Muslims. These were enforced only sporadically but included prohibitions on wearing certain colors of clothing and requirements to wear specific colors so as to be clearly recognizable, prohibitions against building new houses of worship, and a requirement to offer free hospitality to Muslim travelers. The Ottomans did not invent this approach to handling "others" in their midst, for it had already been developed by earlier Muslim empires.

In the Balkans, the vast majority of non-Muslims were Orthodox Christians, with a significant Jewish minority as well as a smattering of Roman Catholics. As far as their internal affairs were concerned, these groups were governed according to what has traditionally been called the *millet* system. Recent scholarship has called into question the use of this term. *Millet,* which means a religiously defined community, does not seem to have been generally applied to non-Muslim groups until the eighteenth century, and *system* implies a strict and centralized structure that never existed. Be that as it may, it is fair to say that the Ottomans mostly left alone those populations who did not see the wisdom of conversion and allowed their internal affairs to be supervised by their own religious authorities under their own laws.

These religious authorities were responsible for seeing that their adherents showed proper respect to the Muslim population, paid their taxes, and caused as little trouble as possible. From the point of view of the Church hierarchy, this system had its advantages, for it allowed clerics to exercise considerably more power over the secular lives of their parishioners than had been the case under the Byzantines. As one eighteenth-century prelate put it approvingly: "In the days of the Christian Empire (alas) . . . prelates administered only the priesthood and ecclesiastical matters and did not intervene in civil matters. . . . Now, however, . . . provincial prelates undertake secular lawsuits and trials, in connection with inheritance, with debts and with almost any aspect of the Christian civil law."[2]

Unfortunately, however, the combination of secular and religious power vested in the clergy led to corruption, particularly at the higher levels. Ambitious clerics learned that they could pay Ottoman officials for the right to hold clerical offices; having attained a high position, they would then commence raising that sum and more from their flock. As the empire became increasingly financially strapped, corruption became endemic, as described colorfully by S. I. Asdrakhas in the eighteenth century:

> And when the chief priest of a diocese dies, immediately the lobbying begins in force, some going to the patriarch, some going to the senior clergy, some to the notables and their wives, and often to the magnates, and of the many one is lucky and receives the office. But as much as he succeeds, many expenses are occasioned by gifts to the go-betweens, some to the Porte, some to the higher clergy, all with i.o.u.s. . . . This new bishop, then, without having 50 *grosia* of his own, falls into an abyss of debt. He comes to the diocese and has no other way of repaying his debts and of holding the high office, with the many expenses and with the many gifts to the *agas* or *pashas* of the region, so that his word will prevail, being strengthened by the Porte with the customary powerful *berat* which reveals him to be the head of the Greeks of the place . . . and with this power, immediately he arrives in the diocese, he begins to seek from the villages help for his new high priestly office of from 50 to 100 *grosia,* from the monasteries of from 100 to 200 *grosia,* from the priests some 10, some 15 *grosia* and so on, all excessive amounts. The poor cannot resist, fearful of excommunications, curses and exclusion from church, the

notables are ashamed of the daily coffee and pipes and gifts. The *agas* do not object, for he says to them: "It is the custom, as my predecessor took it, so do I want it."[3]

Nevertheless, whatever its faults, the millet system did insulate Christians from Muslims and contributed significantly to the long-term survival of the various Balkan peoples. Had the Ottomans attempted to forcibly assimilate the Balkan peoples, they almost certainly could have succeeded, and the result might well have been the disappearance of the Bulgarians, Serbs, and Greeks as distinct peoples. The millet system allowed the Balkan peoples to retain a feeling of separateness and individuality within the fabric of the multiethnic, multireligious empire. When Western European ideas of what a nation should be reached the Balkans in the late eighteenth century, it was often around millet institutions that national identity crystallized.

The position of Jews in the empire differed from that of Christians primarily because the Jewish religion lacked the hierarchy provided by the Christian churches. Communities of Greek-speaking Jews had existed in many cities and towns of the Byzantine Balkans, where they were tolerated if not embraced. After the conquest of Constantinople, and in accordance with Mehmet the Conquerer's plans to repopulate his capital (whose population had shrunk to less than 40,000 by the mid–fifteenth century), the Ottoman authorities compelled most Balkan Jews to leave their homes and move to the capital. They were soon joined by a wave of Jewish emigrants expelled from Spain after 1492. The Greek-speaking Jews had already carved out a central role in trade in Istanbul, and the Spanish-speaking newcomers, because of their broad experience with Western European ways, quickly took up the same activities and expanded them. Indeed, Jewish merchants dominated much of the trade in the Ottoman Empire from the late fifteenth century until the seventeenth century, when they began to be supplanted by Armenians and Greeks. They established large communities, not just in the capital but also in such Balkan cities as Salonika (where they made up 50 percent of the population in the sixteenth century), Edirne, and Sarajevo. Leading Jewish figures, such as Hekim Yakub, a fifteenth-century court physician, and the financiers Don Joseph Nasi and his aunt Dona Gracia Mendes wielded great influence, and they were free to practice and patronize their religion in a way that would have been impossible anywhere else in Europe at the time.

For all its relative tolerance, the Ottoman Empire was emphatically Muslim, however, so it is not surprising that the Balkans, particularly the cities, became heavily Islamic during this period. This occurred to some extent because of a deliberate state policy of forced migration and to a greater extent because of conversion. As had the Byzantines, the Ottomans moved people around the empire. They moved individuals as a form of punishment, or, more frequently, they moved entire populations in an attempt to develop parts of the empire. Thus, not only Jews but also Armenians and Turks from Anatolia were forced to migrate to Istanbul after the conquest. As the capital grew more prosperous, it began to exert a magnetic influence, and in later centuries many people migrated there voluntarily. Large-scale colonization by Muslims at the behest of the authorities also took place in the Balkans, particularly in regions relatively close to Istanbul (today's Bulgaria, northern Greece, and Macedonia). Primarily, these settlers were taken from the Yürüks (nomadic Turkic tribes of Anatolia), but members of other groups, including Tatars and Circassians from the Caucasus, also settled there, further diversifying the population of the peninsula.

More significant than forced migration in the Islamization of the Balkans, however, was conversion. To be sure, the Turks rarely forced conversion on Balkan Christians, with the exception of males taken for the devshirme and a certain number of women and girls who were kidnapped to become wives of upper-class Muslims. Nevertheless, there were obvious blandishments for those willing to convert, and many did so.

Certainly, the upper classes converted more readily than did peasants, as educated and wealthy people had more to lose from intransigence in the face of superior power. As urban dwellers, they interacted more frequently with the Ottoman bureaucrats who had been sent to administer the region, and they could reasonably hope to join the Ottoman elite through conversion. It is less clear, however, why certain ethnic groups (Albanians, Bosnians, and Vlachs) were more inclined to convert than others (Serbs, Greeks, and Bulgarians). It has been suggested, at least in the case of Bosnians, that the relative paucity of parish priests in the pre-Ottoman period caused peasants to be less attached to their religion than was the case for those groups among whom Orthodox clerics were more firmly entrenched. This would certainly have been true among the nomadic Vlachs as well. As for the Albanians, a desire to separate themselves from their Slav neighbors, who, because they were closer at hand, were potentially more threatening than the Turks, probably played a role. It is striking that Albanians and Bosnians were the only Balkan peoples who were already split between Orthodoxy and Catholicism. Perhaps this preexisting split made them more prone to accept another religion. In any case, by the sixteenth century, Islam was firmly entrenched on the Balkan Peninsula. Eventually, some 70 percent of Albanians and 50 percent of Bosnians appear to have converted, while smaller numbers of converts could be found among all other Balkan peoples.

Between the fifteenth and seventeenth centuries, the urban centers of the Balkans became progressively more Islamic. In the fifteenth century, Muslims accounted for some 26 percent of the urban population. By the first half of the sixteenth century, this figure had risen to approximately 40 percent and by the second half of that century to almost 61 percent. Muslim dominance was particularly pronounced in the larger cities. In this regard, the capital, Istanbul, was representative; by the first quarter of the sixteenth century, its population had swelled to some 400,000 inhabitants, of whom 58 percent were Muslim, 31 percent were Christian (mostly Greek speakers), and 11 percent were Jewish (both Spanish and Greek speakers). As elsewhere in the Ottoman Empire, Muslims, Jews, and Christians lived side by side; although they frequently segregated themselves by neighborhood, there were no walled ghettoes in Ottoman cities. In fact, there were no walls at all in the cities the Ottomans founded such as Sarajevo, the new capital of Bosnia. Ottoman control was so firm that no external invaders were foreseen. In the urban landscape, the mosque, rather than the church, became the focus of the neighborhood, although it was characteristic of the most cosmopolitan Ottoman Balkan cities to find mosques, churches, and synagogues in close proximity.

Surprisingly, Ottoman rule and the steady process of Islamization appear not to have had much impact on the economic life of Balkan cities. This was because most Balkan cities were already well formed when the Ottomans arrived, having existed for centuries as the market centers for primarily rural economies, as garrison and administrative posts, and as commercial depots for trade crossing the Balkans between Europe and Asia. Under the Ottomans, as had been the case under Byzantine rule, urban economic life was controlled by guilds, which regulated the production of goods and the provision of services. Taxes on productive and commercial activities provided most of the money required to keep the empire running. Approximately a quarter of the taxes collected in urban areas in the Balkans at the height of the empire, in the mid–sixteenth century, went directly to the support of the sultan, while another half went to support various upper administrative personnel.

The Balkan economy was crucial for the life of the empire as a whole in this period, accounting for almost 40 percent of state revenues, and urban dwellers engaged in a range of activities. In Skoplje (today

European observers, such as Count Luigi Marsigli, an Italian in service to the Habsburgs, were always struck by the prominence of mosques in Ottoman cities. This view of Sarajevo dates to 1697. Author's collection.

the capital of Macedonia) in 1546, for example, the population was quite varied; the largest single group was the city's Turkish garrison (almost 200 people) followed closely by the staff of religious institutions (imams, muezzins, and dervishes). As military, religious, and administrative personnel (*askeri* in Ottoman Turkish), these individuals did not pay taxes. Taxpaying Muslim artisans included some 115 men engaged in various trades related to the production of thread, cloth, and finished clothing, 89 in the areas of shoe and bootmaking, 81 tanners, and smaller numbers of metalworkers, grocers, butchers, carpenters, potters, soapmakers, chandlers, barbers, bathkeepers, merchants, and druggists. Some 50 Muslim males who lived in the city were primarily involved in agriculture. The heads of the 216 Christian households in the city, most of whom appear to have been engaged in agriculture, paid the same taxes as their non-askeri Muslim counterparts, as well as an additional tax required of non-Muslims called the *cizye*.

We know little about how and whether women were employed in Balkan cities under Ottoman rule. According to custom, the wives of wealthier Muslims stayed in the home, out of sight. They often inherited property from relatives and husbands, however, and were able to control it. Ottoman court records provide many examples of women as both litigants and defendants in cases relating to property and inheritance rights, loans, and family matters. In the Balkans, women of less well-to-do Muslim and Christian families were active in the cottage industries that produced thread and woolen cloth, although they were generally not eligible to join the guilds that regulated most aspects of urban economic life. In the countryside, both Christian and Muslim women played a central role, engaging in much of the farm work. In Albania and Bosnia, rural Muslim women usually went unveiled, to the amazement of many later travelers.

Although most of the Balkan Peninsula was under secure Ottoman control, not all the Balkan peoples acquiesced readily even at the zenith of Ottoman power. Those communities that resisted were located mostly at the periphery of the empire or in mountainous regions that were difficult to control. The Albanian Skanderbeg and the Wallachian Vlad III Dracul (Vlad the Impaler) provide two telling examples of resistance. Unlike the Serbs and Bulgarians, Albanian speakers had never succeeded in forming a centralized kingdom in the pre-Ottoman period. The clannish Albanians were led by local lords who spent as much time feuding with each other as they did defending the interests of their subjects.

When the Ottomans reached the southwest Balkans by the early fifteenth century, they had little trouble in subjugating the various Albanian factions, one of which was led by John Castriot. Castriot had been a vassal of Venice but quickly accepted the Ottomans as his overlords and used his ties with them to expand his power. After his death, however, Castriot's lands were seized, a process of dispossession typical for the time. Castriot's son, who had earlier converted to Islam and taken the name of Skanderbeg, rebelled. Having converted back to Christianity, he attempted to unite the Albanian clans against the Ottomans. Between 1444 and his death in 1468, Skanderbeg fought some fourteen campaigns against the Turks. Through his efforts, the mountainous sections of northern Albania remained free, but at enormous cost. Constant military campaigns led to widespread destruction, and by the end of the century, Albania was nevertheless firmly under Ottoman control.

Wallachia was a relatively poor land on the northeastern periphery of Ottoman territory. Like Albania, Wallachia was a borderland whose mostly Orthodox population was threatened by the Catholic Hungarians to the north and west and by Muslim Ottomans to the south. But unlike Albania, whose most fertile land was parceled out as timars in the early fifteenth century, Wallachia remained under the command of its leading aristocrats after Prince Mircea accepted Ottoman overlordship in the late fourteenth century. Vlad II, Mircea's grandson, attempted to play Hungarians off against Ottomans, siding with whoever seemed stronger in order to keep control over his territories. Not surprisingly, neither side trusted him, and when he switched back to the Turks in 1444, he was compelled to send two of his sons, Vlad and Radu, to Anatolia as hostages. After his father's death in 1447, Vlad was set free and made an officer in the Ottoman army. As Vlad III, he ruled Wallachia three separate times, but his most storied reign was his second, which lasted from 1456 to 1462.

Vlad attempted, with ruthless unconcern for human life, to break the power of the local feudal nobility and to create a centralized, absolute state capable of resisting incorporation by more powerful neighbors. Like Skanderbeg, Vlad III broke whatever vows of submission he had taken and led an uprising against the Ottomans in the early 1460s. Ultimately, despite Vlad's undeniable skill as a military commander, tiny Wallachia was unable to muster enough force to counter the Ottoman military machine, particularly since he was unable to convince his neighbors in Moldavia and Hungary to fight at his side. By 1462 Vlad had been hounded out of the country and into Hungarian captivity.

A pamphlet printed in Nürnberg in 1499 shows Vlad the Impaler eating a meal while surrounded by the impaled bodies of his victims. From Hie facht sich au gar ein graussemliche und erschröckenliche hystorien, Strasbourg: Matthias Hupfuff, 1500, from the Nürnberg pamphlet by Ambrosius Huber, 1499.

Outside Romania, where he is considered a protonationalist hero, Vlad is remembered not for his political or military ambitions, but as the prototype for the archetypical vampire. While there is no record of his drinking human blood or sleeping in a coffin, he was an exceptionally cruel and sadistic ruler who instilled terror in enemies and subjects alike. Vlad apparently killed between 40,000 and 100,000 people during his six-year rule, and numerous accounts of his bloodthirsty sprees can be found as early as the fifteenth century, some accompanied by lurid illustrations. As one Ottoman eyewitness put it: "In front of the wooden fortress where he had his residence, he set up at a distance of six leagues two rows of fences with impaled Hungarians, Moldavians, and Wallachians. In addition, since the neighboring area was forested, innumerable people were hanging from each tree branch, and he ordered that if anyone should take one of the hanging victims down, they would hang in their place."[4] It was not until the nineteenth century, however, that Western European writers—most famously Bram Stoker in his novel *Dracula* (1897)—combined ethnographic accounts of Romanian folk beliefs regarding vampires with the historical figure of Vlad to create the modern-day Dracula. This novel can be seen as part of a more general trend in Western Europe in the nineteenth century to see the Balkans as a semiexotic land characterized by savagery and violence.

Despite scattered revolts, Ottoman control over the Balkans from the end of the fifteenth to the end of the sixteenth century was almost total. This permitted the inhabitants of the peninsula to enjoy the longest period of peace since the days of Roman rule; nor were they to experience such sustained internal peace in subsequent centuries. Paradoxically, however, peace did not bring long-term prosperity. Indeed, rather than improving over time, the economic condition of most inhabitants of the Balkans appears to have stagnated or declined from the end of the sixteenth century. There are many overlapping explanations for this. One problem was the state's attitude toward the economy. In the Ottoman Empire, economic activity was supposed to enhance the power of the sultan, and the job of the state was to regulate the economy in order to achieve this aim. As was the case with the Byzantine Empire, stability rather than growth was the central concern. Most important was to ensure an adequate supply of provisions to the cities and a high degree of security for all inhabitants of the empire, each of whom was supposed to remain in his or her carefully regulated place in the hierarchy. In the empire's period of growth, from the fourteenth to the mid–sixteenth century, the system worked reasonably well. Taxes were not overly onerous, and the military could be supported on a combination of taxes generated by timar lands and on profits from conquest.

By the late sixteenth century, however, a number of problems converged to call into question the viability of the Ottoman economy. The empire had now expanded as much as it could, and a lack of new conquests meant that the military was no longer able to support itself. The situation only worsened in the late seventeenth century as the rise of Habsburg power led to a diminution of Ottoman, the loss of the rich Hungarian lands being the biggest blow. As in other parts of Europe in the sixteenth century, the Ottoman Empire witnessed a population explosion. But the Ottoman economic system, designed for stability and continuity, was not sufficiently dynamic to provide economic opportunities for a growing population. Worse, a series of weak sultans proved incapable of exerting control over the empire from the center. The timar system, which did allow for a reasonable standard of living, although it may not have produced rural prosperity, gradually broke down. Local lords began to exert control over the timars, transform them into large private estates, and exploit the peasants unmercifully. By the seventeenth and eighteenth centuries, such local magnates would create powerful fiefdoms that the sultans barely controlled. In some regions peasant farmers began to abandon agricultural land and take to the hills, where they engaged in occupations that were harder to tax, such as stock herding and banditry. These bandits, called Klephts in Greek and Hajduks in Serbian, would later play significant roles in national uprisings against the Ottomans.

Among external factors that contributed to Ottoman decline were the opening of the Americas and the discovery of shipping routes to India and China around the horn of Africa in the sixteenth and seventeenth centuries. With these new trade patterns, the eastern Mediterranean lost its position as crossroads of the world. The empire declined as a shipping center, and enormous revenues were lost. In the Balkans, revenues from mining also diminished, as precious metals looted from the Americas drove the price of local silver below production costs. Although some industries did develop in the Balkans (the weaving of coarse woolen cloth being the largest), the Ottoman Empire did not join in the Industrial Revolution that invigorated the Western European economies in the seventeenth and eighteenth centuries. Perhaps the primary reason for the economic decline was that the Ottoman state continued to resist the market economy; it insisted on regulating prices to ensure that urban centers and the army would be supplied on a regular basis. To be sure, it was not just the Ottoman economy that failed to keep pace with that of Western Europe in this period; this was true throughout the world.

The waning of Ottoman power also brought significant demographic changes, some of which had begun earlier. Greek speakers took advantage of the relatively tolerant attitude of the empire to recolonize the Mediterranean coast of Anatolia, where they came to form the majority of the population. The largest migrations within the Balkans in the Ottoman period, however, involved Serbs and Albanians. The center of Serbia had originally been in Zeta and Raška (roughly today's Montenegro and Kosovo). It remained such through the end of the seventeenth century when the Serbs, heartened by Habsburg gains against the Ottomans in the northern Balkans, rebelled. When the rebellion was put down, some 50,000 Serbs migrated from the former core regions of Serbia north of the Danube, where they were welcomed by the Habsburgs and incorporated into a buffer zone lying between the two empires. The center of Serbia thus shifted northward. Mostly Muslim Albanians moved into the territories vacated by Serbs, and they ultimately became the majority population in much of what had once been Serbia. Serbia's religious center of gravity shifted as well when, after the abolition of the Serbian Patriarchate in Peć (an action instigated by the Greek Orthodox patriarch in Istanbul), a new Serbian patriarchate was established in Habsburg territory in the Fruška Gora region of Vojvodina. In the nineteenth century, it would become a key center for the Serbian national revival.

In addition to long-term economic and demographic legacies, centuries of Ottoman control left a visible imprint on the urban environment of the Balkans and a difficult-to-measure but perhaps even more significant imprint on the daily life of the Balkan peoples. Post-Ottoman governments in the independent Balkan states worked assiduously to "cleanse" their cities of the Ottoman legacy, so it can be difficult to appreciate just how "Ottomanized" these cities once were. Even Athens, however, where today one would have to search far and wide to discover traces of Ottoman presence, was dotted with Ottoman monuments or with religious buildings that, like the Parthenon, had been converted into mosques. Nor did the Ottomans confine themselves to building houses of worship. Major public works projects such as bathhouses, orphanages, hospitals, religious schools, bridges, and the roadside inns called caravansaries marked their presence. Some of these are still used today, such as the bridge in Višegrad, constructed in the 1570s by Mehmet Pasha Sokollu. Until recently, a traveler could still appreciate the specific cosmopolitan feel of an Ottoman city in much of Bosnia,

The multicultural heritage of Sarajevo is evident on postcards such as this one from the late nineteenth century. Writing appears in Cyrillic, Latin, and Arabic scripts, and the buildings depicted in the town center include Austro-Hungarian-era public edifices, Ortho-dox and Catholic churches, and the minarets of the Ferhad mosque. Author's collection.

but during the wars of the 1990s much of the Ottoman architectural legacy was deliberately destroyed.

Far more difficult to root out, however, were the legacies of Ottoman presence in everyday life. A commodity as mundane as coffee, and the rituals for its consumption, reveal the region's Ottoman heritage. The first coffee house in the world opened in Istanbul in the mid–sixteenth century. Later in that century, there were some six hundred cafes in the capital, and the beverage, along with its method of preparation and the places in which it was consumed, had been exported throughout the empire. The poem "Lord, Don't Leave Me without Coffee" by an eighteenth-century Albanian, which is in the form of a prayer, illustrates the importance of coffee.

> By the wonders of the prophets,
> By the saints that we acknowledge,
> Let me break no fast a-thirsting,
> Lord, don't leave me without coffee.
> By the honour of Fatima,
> And Meyreme, don't reject me

With a plate of salty yoghurt,
Lord, don't leave me without coffee . . .
Lord, don't let me break my fast with
Nought to eat but syrup, honey,
Oh God, you are my salvation,
Lord, don't leave me without coffee.
In the Holy Month we're marking,
Please forgive our sins, we're old folk,
By the angels up in heaven,
Lord, don't leave me without coffee.
By the one whose name means mercy,
By Mohammed, fame be to him,
Don't desert me with hulled barley,
Lord, don't leave me without coffee.
To the Lord prays Muçi Zade,
For he wallows in much woe with
Neither rice nor tapioca,
Lord, don't leave me without coffee.[5]

Turkish coffee is prepared in a long-handled pot called a *dzhezva* (the Turkish word is used in almost all Balkan languages) and served, with a healthy dose of sugar, in a small cup accompanied by a glass of water. Until recently, the only coffee available in the region was prepared and served in this manner, although now the ubiquitous espresso machine, imported from Italy, has supplanted the more labor-intensive *dzhezva*. The cafe itself, as the focus of (male) social life, is also originally an Ottoman institution, and the sight of Balkan dwellers hunched over a tiny cup of coffee, smoking a cigarette (another Ottoman innovation), and conversing endlessly is a scene to be savored in any Balkan city or town. Ottoman influence extends to food as well, with such ubiquitous items as baklava, dolmas, and meat kabobs all having been imported to the peninsula by the Ottomans. In many Balkan languages, Turkish words are still used for these and other objects of everyday life.

Finally and most difficult to quantify, Ottoman rule brought with it a set of cultural elements that define what it means to be a "Balkan" type. It is something of a parlor industry in the region to declare that the Balkans begin somewhere immediately to the south or east of one's own home. The point, however, is not where they begin, but that inhabitants of the region, including those who wish themselves out of it, sense that they share some psychological and behavioral characteristics defined as "typically Balkan," including generous hospitality to strangers, tolerance of difference, and a principled refusal to allow the need to make a living interfere with the free and easy patterns of social intercourse.

CHAPTER 4

The Long Nineteenth Century (1775–1922)

In 1775 the Balkan Peninsula was ruled by three empires. The Ottomans still controlled the lion's share, though they had permanently lost Transylvania, Croatia, and Vojvodina to the Austrian Habsburgs by 1774. The Adriatic coast north of Albania was, for the most part, Venetian territory. Exceptions were the small merchant republic of Ragusa (Dubrovnik), whose precarious liberty was sustained by artful diplomacy, and Montenegro, where proud clans eked out a semi-independent existence on mountainous territory too poor to be worth subduing. By 1923, these three empires were a memory, and the political map of the Balkans had been transformed by the appearance of new states named for the peoples who dominated them: Albania, Bulgaria, Greece, Romania, Turkey, and the Kingdom of the Serbs, Croats, and Slovenes. Although nation builders throughout the region proudly pointed to classical and medieval ancestors for the nascent Balkan states, the models on which they were based had actually been imported recently from Western Europe.

Particularly important was the concept of the nation, defined primarily by shared linguistic and secondarily by cultural, historical, and/or religious features, and now perceived as the proper unit around which states should be organized. This view of the necessary congruence between state and nation did not fit comfortably with the political traditions of the region or with the reality of highly diverse communities. In Western Europe, the creation of homogeneous national states proceeded gradually over hundreds of years, from the late Middle Ages through the eighteenth century, and was accompanied by struggles during which individuals and groups opposed to the centripetal forces of nation creation were forcibly assimilated, expelled, or killed. In the Balkans, the same process of homogenization took place relatively swiftly, and it did so under the eyes of Western Europeans who had forgotten, or who chose to overlook, the methods by which they had achieved their own national unity. Rather than seeing the process of Balkan national consolidation in the nineteenth and twentieth centuries as a parallel and somewhat later version of their own history, they began to view the Balkans as a region of constant ethnic conflict inhabited by incomprehensible and semicivilized (though still semi-European) savages.

For almost a millennium, the Balkan peoples had lived within multiethnic, dynastic states. This is not to say that they had no sense of separate identities. On the contrary, they were undoubtedly aware that they and their neighbors spoke a variety of languages, practiced a variety of religions, and lived in a variety of ways. These differences, however, had traditionally been of little importance to the population at large, or to their successive overlords—the Byzantines, the local nobility, and the Ottomans. For local populations, national identities as we now understand them were fluid and would remain so into the twentieth century. Within the Ottoman Empire, the *millet* system, organized on religious principles, cut across other potential markers of identity, including nation, class, and gender. Thus, an Albanian Muslim farmer, a sheep-herding Bulgarian Pomak (as Bulgarian converts to Islam were called), and a rich Bosnian Muslim landowner's wife were all in the Muslim *millet,* while Orthodox speakers of Albanian, Serbian, and Greek would all have been lumped together in the "Roman" (that is, Orthodox) *millet* regardless of their social position or dwelling place.

Much of the population was bi- or multilingual. Indeed, the various Balkan languages, related distantly or not at all, borrowed from each other not only individual words but entire grammatical structures, clear evidence of the exceptional and sustained level of interaction between the various Balkan linguistic communities. In the Ottoman Balkans, Greek was the primary language of culture (not only in Greece, but also in Bulgaria, Romania, and Albania), though Muslims used Arabic, and Serbs employed a heavily Russified form of Old Church Slavic. Ottoman Turkish was the language of cities and the central administration, while trade was carried out in Greek, Venetian Italian, Armenian, and Ladino (the old-fashioned Spanish of the Jewish immigrants from Spain). In Habsburg territories, the language of culture and administration was Latin (until the end of the eighteenth century), and that of business, German. Speakers of what linguists consider a single language could be Muslim, Orthodox, or Catholic, as was the case in both Albania and in Bosnia. Assimilation of one group into another was also common and proceeded in multiple directions as Slavs took on the Albanian language, Albanians became Greek speakers, and Turks assimilated to Slavs. Even religious practice was not pure, with numerous examples of borrowing from Christianity to Islam and vice versa. As a British traveler, Mrs. John Elijah Bunch, noted in a memoir, "Followers of the prophet in Lower Albania especially may be heard to swear alternately by the *Panaghia* (blessed Virgin) and the Prophet, without appearing disposed to follow too closely the doctrines of either the Bible or the Koran."[1]

Premodern political leaders had little difficulty overlooking differences as long as their subjects paid their taxes and fulfilled their service obligations. This was true even at the edges of the Balkans, in Venetian territory, and in the Habsburg Balkan territories, after they had been wrested from the Ottomans in the seventeenth century. Thus, although the Habsburgs were militant Catholics at this time, they extended religious toleration to tens of thousands of Serbian Orthodox settlers because the Serbs provided a permanent military levy to protect the so-called Military Frontier (Krajina) that formed a buffer zone between Habsburg and Ottoman territory.

The first major shock of modernization in the Balkans came in the wake of the French Revolution of 1789 and the subsequent French expansion under Napoleon. All three traditional Balkan imperial powers felt it: the French permanently disbanded the Venetian Republic in 1797, the Ottomans effectively lost control of the rich province of Egypt in the wake of Napoleon's invasion in 1798, and the Habsburgs suffered major military setbacks against French armies in 1804–1805. The French did not actually occupy much of the Balkan Peninsula, contenting themselves with the creation of the "Illyrian" provinces, which included the former Balkan territories of Venice and Dubrovnik (whose independent republic they abolished in 1808) as well as Habsburg territories in Croatia and Slovenia. Proclaiming a political ideology based on the rights of man, and having demonstrated the power of a state whose citizens could be mobilized on the basis of national sentiment, the French made a powerful impression at least on the upper and more educated classes, despite the limited duration of their presence in the Balkans.

The painting reproduced on this book's cover, by the Slovenian artist Johan Krstnik Scherer, is perhaps the most succinct expression of the new ideology. At the center is Napoleon himself, the French revolutionary flag billowing above his head. Napoleon's hand is extended and he is pulling to her feet a woman garbed in a combination of western, peasant, and Turkish clothing, an allegorical representation of the natives of the Illyrian provinces. Broken classical columns, a reminder of the Roman heritage, litter the foreground and the left side of the painting, and in the foreground a youth carves an inscription on a classical fragment: "Illyria reborn by Napoleon's hand." Looking on are, on the right, the French soldiers who made the "rebirth" a reality, and, on the left, a motley crew of "Illyrians," some in European costume, some in the Turkish-inflected dress of the so-called Morlacchi (Dalmatian Slavs).

Even among peoples not directly touched by French rule, revolutionary ideals gained a foothold. Rhigas Velestinlis was one of the earliest of the Balkan natives whose efforts to create independent states in the region led them to be called "national awakeners." In Vienna in 1797, Rhigas published a plan for a future independent Balkan federation inspired by French revolutionary rhetoric. Greek was to be the common language of the proposed federation, but it would include as equal citizens "all the inhabitants of this Empire [the Ottoman], without distinction of religion and speech, Greeks, Bulgarians, Albanians, Wallachians, Armenians, Turks and every other kind of race."[2] This declaration represents an attempt to marry contemporary European political ideas with the multireligious and multiethnic state traditions that the Balkan peoples had inherited from the Romans, the Byzantines, and the Ottomans. Later advocates of independent states in the region would, however, generally ignore traditional models in favor of homogeneous states whose citizens would share a single language and culture. Those who did not would suddenly discover that they had become "national minorities," to be treated as second-class citizens at best, and at worst, forcibly assimilated, expelled, or killed. Rhigas himself suffered the fate of many early Balkan national awakeners. Deported by the Austrians to Ottoman territory, he was executed in Belgrade in 1798.

In 1804, as a direct result of the upheaval caused by the Napoleonic campaigns, the first indigenous Balkan national independence movement began near Belgrade. The situation there had been tense since the late 1790s, when Sultan Selim III attempted to assert control over the Belgrade janissaries, who had, by this time, transformed themselves from a loyal military caste into a quasi-independent band of marauders that supported themselves by preying on the local population. Hoping to control the janissaries and improve conditions for his Balkan subjects, Selim allowed the Serbs to collect their own taxes and form a militia for self-defense against his erstwhile soldiers. When Napoleon invaded Egypt in 1798, however, the Sultan turned his attention away from Serbia. The janissaries returned to Belgrade, killed the local pasha who had been the main defender of Serbian and Ottoman interests, and resumed their depredations.

In response, a group of Serbians under the command of Djordje Petrović (Karadjordje), a successful livestock merchant, began a revolt whose goal was not independence but rather protection from the janissaries and the restoration of the previously granted autonomy. However, the Serbs sought an outside guarantor of their position, and they turned to Orthodox Russia for support, thereby initiating a pattern that would be repeated frequently. Local political movements were never sufficiently strong to achieve their aims on their own, so they invited outside powers to assist. Russia, the Habsburgs, Britain, and France were only too happy to interfere, sometimes in favor of independence movements, sometimes to prop up the Ottomans. Rarely were these interventions for the good of the Balkan peoples. Rather, they usually had the effect of setting one group against another in an attempt to continue the careful balancing act by which the great powers strove to preserve peace among themselves between 1815 and 1914. This was difficult in the Balkans, as each power was actively jockeying for a position of control and influence in a dimly conceived post-Ottoman world. In this instance, as would happen frequently, the outside power proved fickle. At first Russia strongly supported the Serbs, emboldening them to seek not autonomy within the Ottoman Empire but full independence. Russia continued to provide support to Karadjordje until 1812, but when the French invaded Russia, the Serbs were left to their own devices. The revolt collapsed, and Karadjordje and his followers were compelled to flee Serbia in early 1813, thereby ending the first modern attempt at Balkan national independence.

At least as important as political revolutions for the eventual appearance of Balkan states was the parallel process by which the nations that would live in these states were created. It is usually referred to as one of "national rebirth" or "national revival," but these terms are problematic insofar as they imply that national consciousness was a natural phenomenon, already latent among the Balkan peoples. They disguise the fact that at the beginning of the nineteenth century, the putative citizens of Balkan nations were, for the most part, entirely unaware of what nation they belonged to, or even that they belonged to one at all. Such terms also evade the question of why elites in the Balkans were attracted to nation- and state-building projects. After all, if nationhood was always already present, then the work of nation builders was merely to bring it to the surface. This conceals less altruistic motives, including a recognition that national independence would allow the upper and educated classes greater scope to exercise power over their fellow citizens, develop an economy friendly to their interests, and in the case of secularly educated intellectuals, create a forum for the development and appreciation of their talents.

In Western Europe, the inculcation of a sense of national belonging took place over hundreds of years and in many cases was encouraged by independent states that existed before the nation that inhabited them. In the Balkans, the time frame for nation building was compressed, and the absence of local independent states caused the equation to be reversed: here, nations were created first, thanks to the hard work of a handful of European-oriented men; states for these nations came later. The model for Balkan nation builders therefore was not France, but rather Germany, where intellectuals carefully nurtured a sense of national consciousness well before the existence of a unified state. On the German model, the primary definition of a nation was linguistic: a nation was a nation (and could, therefore, hope for an independent political existence in the form of a state) insofar as its citizens spoke a common language. Although Balkan intellectuals and linguists tended to claim that a given language had already existed from time immemorial and thereby provided the necessary glue for a nation, this was generally not the case. Each putative language was in fact comprised of multiple dialects, which often shaded off imperceptibly into dialects of equally ill-defined neighboring languages. Because the vernacular had been used for limited purposes since the Ottoman invasion, much work had to be done to transform these languages into vehicles suitable for a full range of modern administrative, commercial, and cultural purposes. This work proved to be the first step in creating the concept of the nation throughout the Balkans.

The introduction to a Greek grammar published in Paris in 1809 and written by the translator Grigorios Zalikoglou illustrates the primacy of linguistic criteria for national definition in the Balkans:

> Fellow countrymen, we must guard our Language, if we want our nation and our faith to exist vigorously for all time. . . . Myriads of others share the same faith, but not having the same language, will never become one with us. For as long as we preserve uncorrupted this divine language, this sacred fire, the race of Greeks remains immortal, and we, and our descendants, bear the marks of our nobility, that we are the true blood descendants of those who laid the first foundations of the civilization of the human race. . . . Those who do not preserve this language neither dare, nor think of boasting of such ancestors. And not because they believed in the Koran, for neither did Themistocles know the Gospels.[3]

Zalikoglou insists that modern and ancient Greek are the same language, though as the writer of a grammar he must have recognized that there are enormous differences between them. But because he needed linguistic continuity to buttress his claims for the historical continuity of the Greek nation, he overlooked this fact. Although he uses the language of race ("blood descendants"), he excludes anyone who does not speak Greek and includes as a "full-blooded" Greek anyone who does. Finally, language trumps any other potential marker of national identity—thus a Muslim would be considered Greek if he speaks the language, but a Turkish-speaking Orthodox Christian would not be, even if he could prove direct descent from Plato.

Elite agitators for the creation of national languages appeared in all of the Balkan lands during the long nineteenth century. Vuk Karadžić, born in Trsić in Ottoman Serbia in 1787, is an excellent example of the multitalented and hardworking individuals who laid the linguistic and cultural foundations for modern nations in the Balkans. Active as a linguist, lexicographer, ethnographer, writer, and publicist, Vuk almost singlehandedly created a Serbian literary language whose basis was not the Russian-inflected Church Slavic that had previously served as the language of culture among Serbs, but rather what he regarded as the purest form of the spoken Serbian language: his own dialect. Vuk believed that a literature based on this dialect could help to forge a Serb identity that could cross class and religious lines. To propagate his vision of a vernacular Serbian culture, he, with the help of the Vienna-based Slovene linguist Jernej Kopitar, published a Serbian grammar in 1814, a dictionary in 1818, and a translation of the Bible into modern Serbian in 1847. Simultaneously, under the influence of the European, particularly German, fascination with folk poetry, Vuk traveled extensively in Serbia, Montenegro, Croatia, and Bosnia-Herzegovina, transcribing and eventually publishing more than a thousand oral poems of South Slavic bards.

The central importance of language and literature for building Balkan nations cannot be overstressed. When Albanian intellectuals succeeded in agreeing upon a standard literary language in the late 1870s, they enabled the creation of an Albanian nation, despite the fact that Albanians speak two distinct dialects and belong to three religions. Although the existence of a codified language was important, by itself this was not considered proof that a people had attained a level of cultural development sufficient for nationhood. The people of a nation also had to prove that they could produce literary work that would place them among the world's "culture bearers." In many cases, such work was overtly nationalist in character, and a handful of cultural leaders nurtured what can only be called a cult of national literature. They tried to mobilize fellow citizens by using the person and work of the national poet as a source of pride and a rallying point for future political development. Expanded under various regimes—democratic, fascist, communist—these cults still exist. One can find them expressed in the research of respected academics, in textbooks used in schools at all levels, and as part of public political discourse.

For example, Mihai Eminescu, considered the greatest master of the Romanian language, is typical of those Balkan writers who created a body of work around which national high cultures crystallized. Even though his poetic work is highly lyrical and not overtly political, Eminescu is seen as far more than a poet; rather, people regard him as a visionary and critics claim to see in his poetry an "intuition of the future, [an] assembly of mythical echoes, Romanian history and Romanian landscape" and claim that in this work, "the deepest folklore influence coexists as well with ideas assimilated from philosophy, science and *old wisdom.*"[4] This cult of Eminescu has been used as a rallying point for nation building in twentieth-century Romania, as numerous statues, paintings, and memorials to the poet attest.

Nation building is an ongoing task and it requires long-term care and maintenance. If at first it was the somewhat disorganized project of a few intellectuals, after the creation of Balkan states it continued as official government policy. It became a central concern to state educational systems (particularly the teaching of national history and culture), and the supposed "national essence" was woven into such mundane objects as flags, currency and stamps, public symbols such as monuments and tombs, and in the rhetoric employed by political leaders in speeches on national holidays. For Greek nation builders, for example, it was particularly important to connect the modern nation and state with, on the one hand, classical pre-Christian Greek civilization and, on the other, with the Byzantine Empire. Bulgarians and Serbs, by contrast, tended to focus on the glories of their respective medieval states and their long struggle to preserve their Christian heritage during the Ottoman period. Romanians preferred to emphasize the legacy of the Roman Empire.

Following and accompanying the cultural work of nation building was the political task of state formation. In their strivings to create independent states in the Balkans, local elites had to contend not only with the empires who ruled over them, but with neighboring elites intent on forming their own independent states, European powers who frequently used the Balkan peoples as proxies or buffers, and the peasants (the vast majority of their own putative conationals) who generally failed to see why national states would benefit them. The process by which states were created was similar throughout the region. First, a small group of revolutionaries, usually composed of Western-educated, romantically inclined, impractical intellectuals, would lead one or a series of heroic but futile rebellions against the Ottomans. These were generally put down with ease and the leaders captured and executed. But they tended to provoke reprisals by Ottoman soldiers and irregulars against the civilian populations thought to be aiding and abetting the rebels, thereby polarizing the conflict. This in turn encouraged the locals to discover that they did have grievances against the Ottomans that could be satisfied only through the creation of a national state to defend their interests. Simultaneously, massacres of "innocent Christians" were exploited by rebel leaders to draw European powers into the conflict in order to stop the "barbarous Turk." Balkan national liberation movements thus have the dubious distinction of having been the first to recognize that provoking the suffering of their conationals was a good way to elicit external support for their cause.

Vassil Levski, considered the greatest revolutionary hero among the Bulgarians, is typical of the generation of revolutionaries whose lives and deaths inspired nation-building projects in the Balkans. Born in 1837, Levski was originally trained for the clergy. In 1862, however, he fled Bulgaria and joined up with groups that organized a series of insurrections in Bulgarian territory in the 1860s. But by the end of the decade, Levski came to realize that armed intervention by small groups of émigrés would never succeed without the support of the population at large. He returned to Bulgaria and began a clandestine effort to establish local revolutionary committees. In 1872, however, Levski was arrested, and he was executed by the Turkish authorities on February 19, 1873. As the model national hero and martyr, Levski came to be emblematic of the Bulgarian national cause. His execution sparked perhaps the most famous Bulgarian lyric poem ("The Hanging of Vassil Levski" by Hristo Botev), and he has been the subject of innumerable pictures and monuments. Sofia's main soccer team and stadium are named for him, as is the Bulgarian military academy.

Once the flag of national liberation had been raised, populations polarized, and national martyrs created, the cause was taken up by somewhat more practical men and advanced by the great powers of Europe, each of which attempted to cultivate client states in the Balkans. Independence was achieved only gradually. As a rule, a nation was first granted autonomy within the Ottoman Empire, then advanced to being a principality liable to pay tribute, and only later became fully independent. These steps all occurred with the active participation and frequent meddling of the great powers, which not only negotiated the borders of the new states but also provided the constitutional arrangements and even the majority of the monarchs (unemployed members of minor German noble families) for the Balkan states. These new states, however, never contained all the members of a given nation, and therefore the first goal of each was expansion with an eye to incorporating all putative conationals within the state. In Serbia and Greece, for example, a large majority of potential national citizens lived outside the borders of the states created in the first half of the nineteenth century. In the course of that century, both Serbia and Greece would expand several times, but neither was able to achieve its maximal national goals. For Greece in particular, the hope of uniting all Greek speakers in a single state became a national obsession that would lead to tragic consequences in the 1920s. Though less constant in the Serbian political imagination, the project of creating a greater Serbia would remain potent longer and would help to fuel the Balkan conflicts through the 1990s.

Such issues were not exclusive to Greece and Serbia, however. Because of the mixed nature of the populations in the Balkans, almost any territory that one state considered its own tended to be claimed by neighboring states as well. These claims and counterclaims caused significant tension among the new Balkan states, particularly in a number of regional hot spots such as Macedonia (claimed by Greece, Bulgaria, and Serbia), Dobrudja (claimed by Romania and Bulgaria but inhabited, it has been estimated, by more than twenty different ethnic groups in the mid–nineteenth century), Albania (whose territory was claimed by the Albanians themselves but also by Greece and Serbia), and Bosnia and Herzegovina (claimed at various times by Serbia and Croatia). In the nineteenth and twentieth centuries, regional disputes were at various times manipulated by European powers attempting to strengthen their own positions in the region.

Greece and Bulgaria provide contrasting case studies of how national states in the Balkans came into being. The first Greek uprising began in 1821 not in Greece itself but in the Ottoman-controlled Danubian Principalities (today's Romania). A Greek officer in the Russian army, Alexander Ypsilantis, led the revolt, but his quixotic quest ended in failure almost as soon as it had begun. At approximately the same time, however, a group of Greek prelates raised the flag of revolt on the Peloponnesus. Greek forces quickly seized control of the Peloponnesus and some of the islands, but they were unable to drive the Turks out

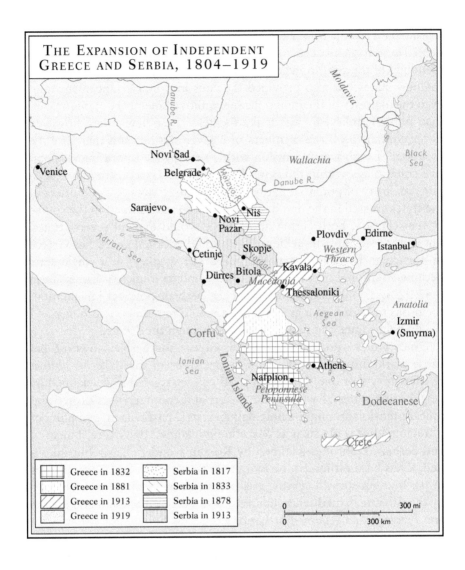

THE EXPANSION OF INDEPENDENT
GREECE AND SERBIA, 1804–1919

Greece in 1832	Serbia in 1817
Greece in 1881	Serbia in 1833
Greece in 1913	Serbia in 1878
Greece in 1919	Serbia in 1913

0   300 mi

0   300 km

completely due to limited resources and internal disputes. In 1825, the sultan called on his erstwhile subordinate, Mehmet Ali Pasha of Egypt, to suppress the revolt, and Mehmet Ali would undoubtedly have succeeded had it not been for the intervention of the European powers. They had been slow to intervene in the conflict, as they were concerned about their own inability to manage a power vacuum in the southern Balkans were the Ottomans to be defeated. But European public opinion eventually demanded support for the Christian Greeks and, in an early instance of "humanitarian intervention," Britain, Russia, and France sent a fleet to protect the Greek rebels in 1827. This fleet destroyed the Turkish-Egyptian navy at the Battle of Navarino. After a great deal of diplomatic maneuvering (as well as a war between Russia and the Ottomans, which took place primarily in the Romanian provinces in 1828–29), the great powers created an independent Greek state that, starting in 1833, was governed by Prince Otho of Bavaria.

The beginnings of the Bulgarian "national revival" lay with church figures. A Bulgarian monk, Father Paisi, working on Mount Athos, wrote a nationalistic history of Bulgaria in 1762 in which he exhorted his countrymen to look with pride on their heritage: "Why are you ashamed to call yourselves Bulgarians, why do you not read and speak your own language?" he asked. "Did the Bulgarians not have their own kingdom and state. . . . Throughout the Slavic world the Bulgarians were the most glorious, they were the first to call themselves Tsars, the first to have a patriarch, the first to be Christianized, they conquered the largest domain."[5] By Father Paisi's day, however, both the Bulgarian language and heritage were under siege, not from the Ottomans, but rather from the Greek-dominated Orthodox patriarchate in Istanbul, at whose urging the Sultan Mustapha III abolished the Serbian patriarchate at Peć in 1766 and the Bulgarian patriarchate at Ohrid in 1767. This placed both Serbian and Bulgarian churches directly under Greek control, but the Bulgarians were more vulnerable because the Serbs had, by the late seventeenth century, created an alternative ecclesiastical center on Habsburg lands. The Bulgarians possessed nothing similar, and the Orthodox patriarch took advantage of his new power to force the Greek language upon the Bulgarian church. In response, beginning in the early 1840s, some church leaders began to agitate for the re-creation of an autonomous Bulgarian church. They sought support from the wealthy Bulgarian merchant community in Istanbul, a group whose leaders also sponsored the first secular schools on Bulgarian territory. By 1866, matters had progressed so far that Bulgarian church leaders expelled Greek bishops from the Bulgarian lands, and in 1872 they proclaimed an independent Bulgarian church.

Political independence, however, proved more difficult to achieve. The 1860s and 1870s had seen a series of failed uprisings, generally led by idealistic, young, European-educated men like Levski. Though often portrayed as heroic rebellions that paved the way for national independence, these insurrections were closer to romantic, albeit dangerous, schoolboy adventures. In any event, a Bulgarian state was created not because of them, but as an outcome of the Russo-Turkish War of

1877–78. That war, and the atrocities connected to it (committed as usual by both sides but blamed in Europe entirely on the Turks), fixed the notion of the barbaric Turk in the European mind and prepared the way for an acceptance of the need to create some form of independent Bulgaria.

The meddling of outside powers in the creation of Bulgaria stands as perhaps the most pernicious external intervention in the Balkans. The terms of the treaty of San Stefano, negotiated between the Russians and the Ottomans and signed in March 1878, created an enormous Bulgarian state. Though not as extensive as the medieval empire of Symeon, it would nevertheless have stretched from the Black Sea almost to the Adriatic and would have given Bulgaria a dominant position in the Balkans as well as dominion over everyone who could remotely be considered a Bulgarian. Such a state, the Russians believed, would be easy to influence and would provide them with a commanding position astride the Balkan Peninsula. From the point of view of the other great powers and that of Bulgaria's Balkan neighbors, a Bulgaria of this size would have been a disaster. Consequently, Russia was forced to submit the treaty for revisions, which were negotiated by all the European powers during the summer of 1878 in Berlin. The proposed Bulgarian state was chopped into three, with the northern section becoming an autonomous principality required to pay tribute to the Ottomans. The southern section, called Eastern Rumelia, was to be a semi-autonomous province under nominal Ottoman control, while Macedonia and Thrace reverted to direct Ottoman rule. The smaller states in the region all acquired some territory as a result of the new treaty, nor were the great powers forgotten: Russia was allowed to annex southern Bessarabia, thereby extending its territory to the mouth of the Danube, while Austria-Hungary, which feared Serbian expansion, was permitted to create a protectorate over Bosnia and Herzegovina (which it would officially annex in 1908).

The Treaty of Berlin was a compromise that pleased no one, and the entire political history of the southern Balkans between 1878 and the end of World War I was an extended attempt to change its provisions, often by violence. The wrangling in the wake of the treaty revisions led to a realignment of European alliances, with Russia, France, and Britain finding themselves on one side and Germany, Austria-Hungary, and the Ottomans on the other. The tensions between these two blocs would simmer until 1914, when events in the Balkans would trigger World War I. For the Balkan states, the central outstanding issue was Macedonia, coveted by Bulgaria, Greece, and Serbia.

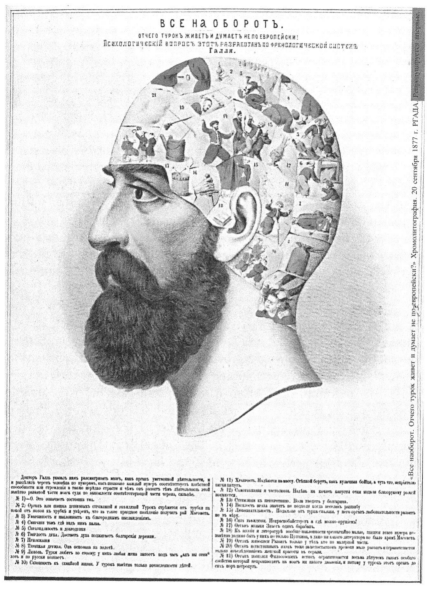

This illustration from a Russian periodical is an excellent example of the anti-Turkish propaganda that circulated throughout Europe at the time of the Russo-Turkish war of 1877–78. The heading reads, "Everything Backwards. Why the Turk Neither Lives nor Thinks Like a European! This Psychological Question Answered Using the Phrenological System of Gall." The various caricatures present an absurdly stereotyped picture accusing Turks of being biologically prone to violence and uneducable. Rodina Magazine, *author's collection.*

Before the Bulgarians could worry about Macedonia, however, they needed to consolidate their own state under the rule of Prince Alexander of Battenburg, who was chosen to rule the country by the European powers. By 1885, despite the objection of the Europeans, Eastern Rumelia merged with Bulgaria, undoing at least part of the Treaty of Berlin. The Macedonian question remained open, however. The inhabitants of this small but strategically vital province were, even by Balkan standards, a mixed lot, including a majority of Slavic speakers but also generous numbers of Greeks, Albanians, Turks, and Roma. In the last decades of the nineteenth century, the three surrounding states aggressively asserted their claims to the territory, attempting to convince the outside world, and the Macedonian inhabitants themselves, that Macedonians were, in fact, Bulgarians, Greeks, or Serbs. Within Ottoman-controlled Macedonia, a group called the Internal Macedonian Revolutionary Organization (IMRO) appeared, whose members foresaw a separate Macedonian identity. IMRO led the bloody and unsuccessful Ilinden uprising in 1903, the last in the series of Balkan revolutions against the Ottomans.

A solution to the Macedonian issue was ultimately achieved, not by the Macedonians themselves but in the course of two brief, bloody Balkan Wars in 1912 and 1913. In the first, Greece, Bulgaria, Serbia, and Montenegro, having agreed beforehand on how Macedonia was to be divided, attacked the remaining Ottoman Balkan territories. They routed the outnumbered Ottoman troops with ease but were unable to agree among themselves as to who should occupy what. Bulgaria, which felt itself most aggrieved by the postwar division of Macedonia, attacked Greece and Serbia in late June 1913. The results were disastrous for Bulgaria, which soon found itself at war not only with its neighbors to the west but also with Romania, Montenegro, and the Ottomans. When the dust had settled, Bulgaria was compelled to sign the Treaty of Bucharest, by which it ceded large amounts of territory to each of its neighbors. The big winners were Serbia, Montenegro, and Greece. Albania, the final Balkan nation-state to appear during the nineteenth century, was also created by the provisions of this treaty.

By the end of the long nineteenth century, the majority of the Balkan peoples lived in national states created on European models with much intervention of the great powers. The upper and educated classes had consolidated their national languages and cultures and begun the task of creating citizens imbued with a national consciousness. At the same time, the Balkan countries shared many features that differentiated them from Western European states. The lack of harmony between national and state boundaries was one significant feature that marked the region. The populations of most states were far more heterogeneous than those of most of their European counterparts, and many potential conationals lived outside of the nation state, either in other, competing Balkan states or in territories that remained part of the Ottoman Empire or Austria-Hungary. Nor were the economies of the Balkan states similar to those of Western Europe. Whereas, by the end of the nineteenth century, industrialization and urbanization were well advanced in Western Europe (even in relatively late-starting economies such as Italy and Germany), these processes had barely gotten underway in the Balkans. Cities were tiny, both in the former Ottoman lands and in those territories that were still part of the Austro-Hungarian Empire. Zagreb, the capital of Croatia, had barely 75,000 inhabitants in 1910, and only five other cities in Croatia-Slavonia could boast a population of even 10,000. The population of Athens in 1880 was less than 70,000, and that of Belgrade less than 25,000 in 1866. The situation in Bulgaria was similar, with the centers of Sofia and Varna each having fewer than 15,000 inhabitants according to the Ottoman census of 1866.

Like all the Balkan capitals, Tirana, Albania, was not very urban in 1918, as this photograph of a central square reveals. Here, mountain tribes bring their cattle and their wood-laden pack donkeys to market. National Geographic.

A story about the Serbian nation-builder Vuk Karadžić and his Croatian counterparts Ljudevit Gaj and Ivan Mažuranić provides a telling illustration of the enormous gulf that separated European-educated, nationally oriented elites and illiterate peasants. The three were traveling together in Dalmatia, trying to ascertain the national feelings of the local population. They approached a man and asked him to say who he was. He replied that he was "a Dalmatian and that he spoke 'our language.'" Later he amended this to say that he spoke "Slavic." At this, Karadžić became exasperated and asked the man whether he had ever heard of Serbian. When the man said no, Karadžić asked whether the man understood him and, having received an affirmative answer, informed the peasant that they were speaking Serbian to each other. Then Mažuranić asked whether he had heard about Croatian. The man purportedly replied, "Oh, that's what I forgot about; we are Croatians and speak Croatian."[6]

The question "who are you" simply did not mean the same thing to the peasant as it did to his enlightened interlocutors. His first answer, "Dalmatian," was both a geographic and political one—the space in which they found themselves was called the province of Dalmatia by the Austrian authorities. But Dalmatia to this man was not a linguistic category because he spoke not "Dalmatian" but "our language," which presumably included both his own dialect as well as the different dialects of Karadžić and Mažuranić. Even his final answer appears not to have been spontaneous but rather a recollection of something he had been told (perhaps by previous enlighteners). And insofar as he felt himself to be a Croat, this identity was not defined, as would frequently be the case in later periods, in opposition to a Serbian identity of which he had apparently never heard. In sum, his worldview was not that of a European-educated man but rather reflected an earlier reality in which identity was simultaneously more local and more ecumenical than it would become.

A graphic illustration of this problem can be seen in the plates of a British travelogue published in 1866, which provides an excellent vision of what European-oriented elites were up against as they tried to form modern states and national identities in the region. The illustration contrasts traditionally clad Bulgarian peasants, oblivious to the presence of outsiders in their midst, a young man with a European education, and a merchant playing the traditional role of mediator between the parochial peasants and the outside world.

The vast majority of the people whom the "enlighteners" were trying to reach in the Balkan countries were illiterate and involved in agriculture (from some 75 percent of the population of Slovenia to 90 percent

In the foreground is a quartet of Bulgarian peasants in traditional dress. They are quite engrossed in discussing their own business, taking no notice of the on-looking outsiders. At center is a merchant, a figure who often acted as an interces-sor between the parochial peasants and the outside world. Behind him, completely marginalized, is his European-educated son, who looks on with a mixture of disdain and bewilderment. From G. Muir Mackenzie and A. P. Irby, *Travels in the Slavonic Provinces of Turkey-in-Europe*, London: Alexander Strahan, 1866.

in Albania). In the case of Romania, large estates were oriented to capitalist farming, producing grain for export to both Western Europe and
the Ottoman Empire. In Ottoman territory, some large estates (primarily
in Macedonia and Thrace) also produced crops for export, including
opium, cotton, and tobacco. In Serbia, agricultural exports, almost all
to Austria-Hungary, took the form of livestock on the hoof. But most
Balkan peasants were involved in semisubsistence farming on relatively
small plots, practically insulated from the cash economy. Through the
middle of the nineteenth century, population densities were low, ensuring
a minimum level of subsistence in rural areas. Toward the end of the century, however, overpopulation in rural areas had become a problem. This
did not lead to a jump in urban populations, however, which remained
tiny throughout the region. Rather, the chief export crop from the Balkan countries at the turn of the twentieth century was often people, with
hundreds of thousands of young men, and a smaller number of women,
immigrating to the United States and, later, to Australia, Canada, and
South America.

Peasant families in the core Balkan regions tended to live in extended groups (the so-called *zadruga*), which ranged in size from relatively rare groups numbering more than fifty, to more common arrangements of a dozen or two consisting of husband, wife, children (married and unmarried), and the children's wives and children all under a single roof. The zadruga held its arable land and livestock in common, with economic decisions made by the male leader. As Olive Lodge, a British aid worker in Serbia, wrote in *Peasant Life in Jugoslavia*,

> The *domaćin* [as the male head of household was called in Serbia] organizes the work of all the members of the family, deciding who shall go ploughing, or hoeing, or to market. He also gives out the wool, cotton, or hemp for weaving, settles when new clothes are necessary, or when sandals (*opanci*) must be bought, and gives out money for purchases. He also chooses which women shall stay at home; but his wife (*domaćica*), as head of the women, allots the household tasks. She also consults with the women with regard to the washing, weaving, and embroidery that should be completed during their periods of work at home, though each woman really needs little or no direction.[7]

Illiteracy was practically universal in the countryside, and even in the cities, institutions of higher education were almost completely absent (the University of Zagreb, founded in 1874, is the oldest in the Balkans). As a result, ambitious young men (and the occasional woman) were forced to pursue their studies in Vienna, Prague, St. Petersburg, or Paris, rather than in their own countries. Modern transportation links in the region were rudimentary at best, with rail lines particularly underdeveloped. This was the result not only of the inability of the small Balkan kingdoms to attract the foreign investment capital needed to lay rail lines, but also because local and great power political rivalries in the region hindered the creation of international lines through multiple countries. Even within the lands of Austria-Hungary, there was poor coordination between those sections administered by Hungary and those ruled directly from Vienna.

Taken together, then, on the eve of World War I, the Balkan lands formerly under Ottoman rule had achieved political independence and possessed small, educated elites who had produced an impressive high culture. At the same time, these states were politically immature, poor, and underdeveloped in comparison to their Western European counterparts, jealous of their neighbors' territories, and vulnerable to the machinations of the powers that surrounded them. The parts of the Balkans under Habsburg rule were likewise poor and underdeveloped in comparison to Western Europe, and the mostly South Slavic–speaking populations felt increasingly disenfranchised in an empire that seemed to favor its Germanic and Hungarian elements. The independent kingdom of Serbia was a powerful magnet for many young Slavs of Austria-Hungary who became intrigued at the possibility of a unified South Slav state (Yugoslavia, which means "south Slavic state" in Slavic languages), and a group of such young men formed the core of the Mlada Bosna (Young Bosnia) movement. With active support from rogue elements in the Serbian armed forces, they assassinated Archduke Franz Ferdinand, heir to the throne of Austria-Hungary, on June 28, 1914, the 525th anniversary of the Battle of Kosovo.

World War I was the logical culmination of nineteenth-century political and military developments on the Balkan Peninsula. For decades the European great powers had upheld a precarious balancing act, employing the fractious Balkan peoples as proxies. But when Austria-Hungary used Serbia's involvement in Franz Ferdinand's assassination to declare war, the Balkan "powder keg" finally blew up. For Europe, World War I would have devastating consequences far beyond the redrawing of the political map. An entire worldview, predicated on the belief that human civilization, embodied by Europe, was making progress in all areas and had outgrown its primitive tendency to destroy itself through violence, was obliterated by more than four years of unprecedented bloodletting. The Balkans were an important battleground, which began with Austria-Hungary's attack on Serbia in August 1914 and effectively ended with the breakthrough of Allied forces on the Salonika front in the fall of 1918. Although not all the Balkan countries took part initially, by war's end, all with the exception of Albania (where central authority simply melted away) had allied with one side or the other, in most cases choosing to fight with whichever side promised to allow them to harmonize the borders of state and nation after the conclusion of hostilities.

At the beginning of the conflict, Serbian forces fought with surprising vigor, repulsing Austro-Hungarian attacks. But when Bulgaria, which had been promised its San Stefano borders by the Central Powers (Austria-Hungary and Germany), opened a second front against Serbia in October 1915, the Serbian military collapsed; the remnants of the army together with the government were forced into a harrowing wintertime evacuation through Albania to Corfu. Romania also waited to see which side would offer the greatest concessions. Prime Minister Ion Bratianu wanted guarantees that Transylvania, a part of Hungary but containing a large Romanian-speaking population, would be ceded to Romania after the war. Having received such promises from the Allies

(Britain, France, and Russia), Romania joined the fighting in August 1916. It quickly became clear, however, that Romania could not stand up to the German and Austro-Hungarian military. Romania capitulated to the Central Powers in December 1917, seemingly losing any chance to gain Transylvania but promised instead Bessarabia, whose Romanian-speaking population had been ruled by Russia. Greece was the final Balkan nation to enter the war, prevented from doing so earlier by wrangling between the pro-German King Constantine and the pro-Allies prime minister Eleutherios Venizelos. Eventually, the Allies compelled Constantine to abdicate, and Venizelos, whose government was centered in Salonika, brought Greece into the war on the Allied side.

World War I led to the military defeat and disappearance of a number of the great powers. Russia was the first to collapse. Although the architects of the February 1917 revolution that toppled Tsar Nicholas II promised to keep Russia in the war, the Bolshevik coup of October 1917 led to the withdrawal of Russian forces from the Allied war effort and to a sharp contraction of Russian influence on Balkan developments. After the rout of the Austro-Hungarian, German, and Bulgarian forces in northern Greece in the fall of 1918, Austria-Hungary disintegrated as well, leaving a power vacuum in the northern part of the Balkan Peninsula. The end of the war also saw the death throes of the Ottoman Empire. Although the last sultan would not formally abdicate until 1922, the birth of Turkey as a modern and secular nation-state had already begun under the leadership of Mustafa Kemal (Atatürk) in 1920.

The disappearance of the external powers that had exerted such a strong influence over the region had major implications for all of the Balkan states. Perhaps the most strongly affected was Serbia, which found itself by November 1918 in control of all the lands on which Serbs lived as well as most territories with a South Slavic population except Bulgaria. There had for some time in Serbia been disagreement as to whether the national goal should be the unification of all Serbs or rather of all South Slavs (except Bulgarians, who already had their own state). The state of affairs after the war led almost inexorably to the latter goal. On December 1, 1918, at the request of a delegation from the National Council of Zagreb (representing the South Slavs formerly in Austria-Hungary), Serbian Crown Prince Aleksandar Karadjordjević proclaimed the creation of the Kingdom of the Serbs, Croats, and Slovenes. Though all three groups seemed satisfied with this arrangement, they had quite different reasons, and these would soon plague the fledgling Yugoslav state. For the Serbs, the incorporation of all Serbian

Mustafa Kemal (Atatürk) in 1924, shortly after he became president of the new Turkish Republic. In this portrait, he wears a traditional Turkish nomadic hat, but one of his reforms, in an effort to Westernize Turkey, was the banning of the fez. Library of Congress, LC-USZ62–98329.

speakers had always been the central goal. Many Serb intellectuals felt a strong affinity for their fellow Yugoslavs, but senior Serbian military and political leaders were not entirely happy to live in a single state with peoples who had, after all, fought loyally for Austria-Hungary during the war. Certainly, they tended to see themselves as senior partners in the kingdom and to mistrust the former Habsburg subjects, including those Serbs who had lived in Austria-Hungary.

As for the Croats and Slovenians, their leaders had long held ambivalent views about Serbia. On the one hand, they admired the Serbs for having achieved independence. Already in the 1830s, one group of Croatians, the "Illyrianists," agitated for the creation of a common South Slav nation and encouraged the development of a unified Serbo-Croatian language in order to bring this about. Movement toward amalgamation with Serbia, however, was counterbalanced by the efforts of various political groups, including factions that advocated greater unity with the Hungarians (who controlled most of Croatia after 1867) and those supporting a more narrow Croatian identity. Slovenes were even less inclined to South Slav unity, in part because their language was fairly distant from Serbo-Croatian and also because their leading political figures were clerics whose orientation tended toward Catholic Vienna rather than Orthodox Belgrade. What tipped the balance in 1918 for both groups and induced them to support a unified South Slav state was the fear that Italy—which had joined the Allied war effort precisely because it had been promised territorial concessions in Dalmatia and Slovenia—would seize much of their territory if they did not join a larger entity. The Croats and Slovenians hoped, however, that this new state would not merely be a larger version of Serbia (though they agreed to a Serbian king) but rather a decentralized state that would satisfy the aspirations of all its citizens.

By 1918, most of the Balkan Peninsula had been at war for six years. Bulgaria, which had a prewar population of some 5 million, lost 160,000 men with an additional 400,000 wounded. Serbian losses were even more catastrophic: of a population of some 3 million, military deaths amounted to approximately 300,000, and perhaps 500,000 civilians died as well. The fighting also created large numbers of refugees and destroyed much of whatever basic infrastructure the Balkan states had managed to build. Finally, postwar political readjustments led to further economic disruption. The new Kingdom of the Serbs, Croats, and Slovenes needed to harmonize incompatible railway, legal, and monetary systems that had been inherited from Austria, Hungary, the Ottoman Empire, and the prewar Serbian state. Even had all parties acted with the best of intentions and had resources been abundant (neither of which was the case), this would have been a titanic task. Bulgaria, which had already been one of the poorest Balkan countries, was required by the terms of postwar treaties to pay backbreaking indemnities to its victorious neighbors. Albania, which had for all intents and purposes disappeared during the war, had to begin the process of state creation from the ground up on a land with few economic resources.

Though Greeks were for the most part spared from fighting on their own territory, the dream of a greater Greece that would incorporate all Greek speakers into a single state led to a disastrous postwar military adventure. According to the Treaty of Sèvres in 1920, the Ottoman Arab territories were to be divided between Britain and France. The British encouraged the Greeks to expand their presence in Asia Minor (they were supposed to control only the area directly around the port of Smyrna), and in 1921 Greek forces drove far into mainland Turkey

Wars, border changes, and "ethnic cleansing" led to massive refugee flows throughout the Balkan region especially from the late 1870s until World War I. In this 1913 photograph, long lines of Turkish refugees fleeing the Balkan wars arrive in Istanbul. In many cases, the families of these "repatriated" Turks had been living in the Balkans for hundreds of years. The caption to the National Geographic photo, "The Turk goes out of Europe as he came," reveals a total lack of sympathy for these refugees. National Geographic.

in an attempt to consolidate their hold over areas with sizeable Greek-speaking populations. In 1922, however, they were routed by Turkish forces. This military debacle led to the loss of all Greek-held territory in Asia Minor as well as the practical elimination of Greek presence in those lands. By the terms of the Treaty of Lausanne (1923) signed by Greece and Turkey, a supervised "population transfer" compelled more than 1 million Greek speakers to leave their homes in Turkey (in some cases lands their families had inhabited for more than a thousand years) and "return" to Greece. In exchange, some 400,000 Turkish speakers were "repatriated" to Turkey.

The nineteenth century in the Balkans was marked both by innovation, including the appearance and consolidation of national cultures and the creation of independent national states, and by continuity, especially in the rural conditions in which the bulk of the peninsula's inhabitants lived. In this period, the region also became *the Balkans,* a specific and problematic area both in the minds of Western Europeans, who tried to understand and control the emerging Balkan nations and states, and among local elites themselves as they struggled to refit Balkan reality to European-style political models. By the measures of political institutions and high culture, they had succeeded fairly well by the end of the nineteenth century.

Economically and socially, however, the Balkan states were far less developed than those of Western Europe. What is more, they remained highly heterogeneous in terms of national composition, with minorities making up some 25 percent of the total population in some states. The gap between relative political and cultural advancement and socioeconomic backwardness (in European terms, of course) in the new Balkan states was painfully obvious to better-educated and better-off citizens. They would struggle throughout the twentieth century to "catch up" to Western Europe.

CHAPTER 5

The Twentieth Century: From the Balkans to Southeast Europe

As Balkan societies were increasingly drawn into the European and world economies in the course of the twentieth century, urbanization, mass education, secularization, and industrialization eroded and ultimately overwhelmed traditional peasant cultures. When the American classicist Milman Parry traveled through Yugoslavia in the 1920s and 1930s, he recorded the singing of illiterate bards whose techniques dated back, in his view, to the days of Homer, but a traveler in the 1980s would have been more likely to encounter local rock bands singing American favorites. The twentieth century also saw the gradual disappearance of the extraordinary ethnic and cultural diversity that had been characteristic of the region for a millennium. With the exception of Yugoslavia, all the Balkan states had become essentially monoethnic by the 1950s, thereby losing much of their specifically Balkan character. With the collapse of multiethnic Yugoslavia in the 1990s and the creation of more or less homogeneous successors over most of its territory, the Balkans, in the traditional sense, would cease to exist. Finally, the end of the century saw the Balkan region begin to lose its traditional borderland position. The rapid integration of most countries in the region into pan-European and trans-Atlantic institutions such as NATO and the European Union indicates that twentieth-century developments transformed the Balkans from an exotic, thoroughly marginal, semicolonialized third world into an integral part of Europe.

Although the social and economic processes of modernization spanned the entire twentieth century, in political terms, the century breaks into two distinct halves and a coda, each dominated by a major European political ideology: the 1920s and 1930s fell under the shadow of fascism, the period from 1945 until 1991 was marked by communism, and developments since 1991 are unfolding against the backdrop of European integration. The political trajectories of the Balkan states in this period were remarkably similar. Each began the 1920s under a democratic parliamentary government. Three—Romania, Bulgaria, and the Kingdom of the Serbs, Croats, and Slovenes—were constitutional monarchies, whereas Greece became a republic after 1923, as did a reconstituted Albania. In each state, parliamentary democracy was abrogated and replaced by a right-wing, though not specifically fascist, dictatorship under a leader who pledged to preserve the nation from internal chaos and external danger. By the late 1930s, these dictatorships tried to come to some kind of accommodation with fascist Italy and Nazi Germany, if only in the interests of economic and territorial self-preservation. After World War II, the Balkan states, with the exception of Greece, found themselves under communist rule. Since 1991, the former communist states have moved toward democratic government and the market economy, though they have done so at different rates, depending on internal political and social conditions.

The experience of Greece typifies Balkan political developments in the interwar period. As World War I ended, King Constantine, whose pro-German position had left him discredited, was compelled to leave the country. A 1924 plebiscite confirmed this decision; some 70 percent of voters opted for a republic. The political situation remained extremely unstable, however, until 1928, when Eleutherios Venizelos returned from abroad to become Prime Minister and head of the powerful Liberal Party. Given the experience of Western Europe, where few leading political figures were able to bridge the pre- and postwar worlds, it may seem surprising that Venizelos could return to lead his country after an eight-year hiatus. But this political trajectory was not unusual in the Balkans, where political continuity was the rule. Thus, the Kingdom of the Serbs, Croats, and Slovenes was headed by the Karadjordjević dynasty that had been on the Serbian throne since 1903. The most powerful political party in the new state, the Radicals, had been under the leadership of Nikola Pašić since 1888. In Romania, Ferdinand ascended the throne in 1914 and remained head of state until his death in 1927. The liberal party that dominated the Romanian political scene in the 1920s was headed by Ion Bratianu, whose father had been the central political figure in Romania in the 1870s and 1880s. In Bulgaria, the ruling dynasty remained in power as well, though King Ferdinand, widely blamed for the Bulgarian military disasters of the second Balkan War and World War I, was forced to abdicate in favor of his son Boris. Here, however, a major new political leader appeared, Alexander Stambuliski, whose Agrarian Party received overwhelming support in the immediate

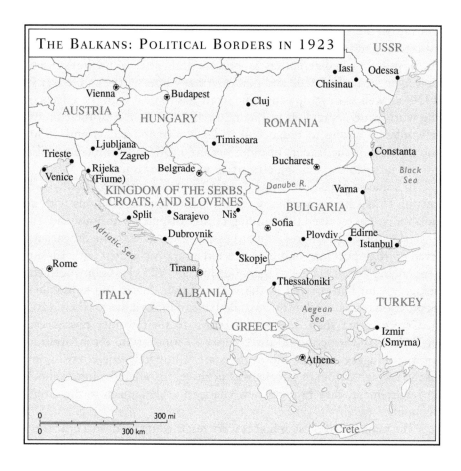

THE BALKANS: POLITICAL BORDERS IN 1923

postwar period. Only Albania saw complete political change. Two leaders emerged: the liberal Bishop Fan Noli, who had risen to prominence among the émigré Albanian Orthodox community in the United States, and the more conservative Muslim Ahmet Zogu. Zogu would force Noli from power by 1925 and then go on to dominate Albanian politics until World War II.

Political continuity in this turbulent period was a sign of stability, but it also meant that the leaders of the postwar Balkan countries had developed their worldviews in a very different time. In the context of the 1920s, their ideas were often out of date, and these leaders, for the most part advanced in age, proved incapable of dealing with the complexities of both the local and European situations. One of the most crucial local concerns was the need to integrate significant new populations in all the Balkan states except Albania. At the same time, the Balkan states had to develop political and military strategies to counter the threat posed by belligerent fascist powers (Italy after Mussolini's rise to power in the early 1920s and Nazi Germany after Hitler's takeover in 1934) as well as develop economic strategies to deal with the effects of the worldwide depression beginning in 1929. Still, for all their faults, it would be wrong to judge Balkan leaders of the 1920s and 1930s too harshly, as the leaders of more mature European democracies also proved incapable of dealing effectively with these issues.

In some respects, the Greek leader Venizelos was remarkably successful. Under his leadership, Greece cultivated good relations with its neighbors. He resolved outstanding border disputes with Italy and Yugoslavia and made progress toward easing tensions with the Bulgarians. Even more important, Venizelos effected a rapprochement with Turkey, renouncing Greek claims to the lands lost in 1923. This convinced the refugees who had arrived in the wake of that defeat and subsequent population exchange that they would have to make a life for themselves in Greece rather than dream of a return to their former possessions in Turkey, and it permitted the country to concentrate on incorporating the refugees into the life of the state. Ultimately, the contribution of the former Ottoman Greeks was positive, for after the initial shock of resettlement, they brought new energy and dynamism to the Greek economy.

The majority of these refugees were resettled on lands in Thrace and Macedonia vacated by Turkish and Bulgarian speakers who had been "repatriated" as part of the postwar agreements, and most of the rest ended up in and around Athens. The demographic effect of the refugees was significant, especially in Greek Macedonia, which went from being a "typically Balkan" province—with a mixed population of Turkish, Slavic, Vlach, and Roma speakers alongside a Greek-speaking population that constituted less than 45 percent of the whole in 1912—to one in which 88 percent of the inhabitants were Greek speakers in 1926.

Although the refugee problem caused massive headaches for the Greek government, the exchange of populations, despite the enormous short-term suffering it caused, did provide some long-term benefits for Greece and Turkey. In the context of newly formed European-style nation-states, which were simply unable to accept the presence of large numbers of others in their midst, it is difficult to imagine that Greeks and Turks would have managed to avoid future conflict over their minority populations had the population exchanges not occurred. The example of Cyprus, where clashes between the two groups remained a problem until the partition of the island in 1974, indicates what might have happened if the two countries had not agreed to eliminate the variety that had characterized them in the past. Nevertheless, the population exchanges led to cultural impoverishment for both countries, as possibilities for vibrant exchange that had characterized the region were suddenly cut off. This tradeoff would characterize each of the Balkan countries in the twentieth century.

The refugee issue in Greece points to a shared concern of all the Balkan states save Albania in the interwar period, but Greece's overall positive experience with new populations was not repeated elsewhere. Bulgaria, for example, faced a much thornier problem, though its refugee burden was smaller. Unlike Greece, which gave up its territorial dreams, Bulgaria remained unwilling to abandon the desire for the Macedonian lands promised at San Stefano, temporarily gained during World War I, and lost again in the peace settlements. The country was, in a way, held hostage by some 250,000 Macedonian refugees, most of whom lived close to the border with Yugoslavia. Their belligerent political organization, IMRO, played a malevolent role in interwar Bulgarian politics. With the majority of Macedonia having been awarded to Yugoslavia, which immediately began a campaign to Serbianize the region, IMRO agitated for Bulgarian intervention. Bulgarian prime minister Stambuliski, recognizing that Bulgaria would be better off having good relations with its neighbors, tried to suppress IMRO. Not surprisingly, therefore, IMRO guerrillas participated happily in the 1923 coup that ousted him, and he was murdered by their fighters. For the next decade, IMRO operated as a kind of state within a state. IMRO terrorists assassinated Bulgarian leaders who wished to improve relations with Greece and Yugoslavia in addition to carrying out cross-border terrorist attacks, and an IMRO gunman assassinated Yugoslavia's King Aleksandar during a state visit to France in 1934.

The problems of new populations in postwar Romania and Yugoslavia were even more complex than in Bulgaria. Romania expanded enormously after the war, and the new country of Yugoslavia incorporated not only the entire Serb population (no matter how defined) but practically all of the South Slavs of the former Austro-Hungarian lands. Thus, both the Serbs and Romanians had achieved their respective nineteenth-century dreams: the incorporation of almost all their conationals into a single state. At the same time, dreams fulfilled led to new problems. Unexpectedly, internal relations between these populations were rocky, for there turned out to be much distrust between the inhabitants of the former independent kingdoms and the "redeemed"

Serbs and Romanians who had been living in Austria-Hungary. The latter expected to live in a state much like the former multinational empire, which gave the regions a great deal of autonomy, but politicians from the former pursued policies of centralization around the old capital. This effectively privileged the elites of the preexisting national states at the expense of former Habsburg citizens, who were often perceived as overly cosmopolitan and not sufficiently patriotic. They in turn tended to look down on the "national" elites as boorish and uncultured.

Relations with minorities, however, were even more problematic. The history of settlement within multinational empires in which nationality had not played an important role guaranteed that a state that included all Serbs or all Romanians would also include large numbers of non-Serbs and non-Romanians (unless, of course, population transfers or expulsions were to be used to rid the state of minorities). Postwar Romania contained a minority population of almost 25 percent, including some 8 percent Hungarians (primarily in Transylvania) and some 5 percent each of Jews, Ukrainians, and Germans. Hatred toward these minorities, particularly Jews and Hungarians, was broad and deep, making Romania fertile ground for home-grown, right-wing groups by the late 1920s and 1930s. Chief among these was the Iron Guard, the only truly popular fascist movement in the Balkans, which was led by the charismatic Corneliu Zelea Codreanu. Combining fervent nationalist rhetoric, religious messianism, and vitriolic anti-Semitism and anti-Hungarianism, the Iron Guard became a leading political force in Romania by the second half of the 1930s, attracting not only the downtrodden but many of Romania's leading intellectual figures as well.

The memories of Nicholas M. Nagy-Talavera provide a feeling for the charismatic presence of Codreanu:

> There was suddenly a hush in the crowd. A tall, darkly handsome man, dressed in the white costume of a Romanian peasant, rode into the yard on a white horse . . . his childlike, sincere smile radiated over the miserable crowd, and he seemed to be with it yet mysteriously apart from it. Charisma is an inadequate word to define the strange force that emanated from this man. He was more aptly part of the forest, of the mountains, of the storms on the snow-covered peak of the Carpathians, and of the lakes and rivers. And so he stood amid the crowd. . . . An old whitehaired peasant woman made the sign of the cross on her breast and whispered to us, "The Emissary of the Archangel Michael." Then the sad little church bell began to toll, and the service, which inevitably preceded Legionary meetings, began.[1]

In calling itself the Kingdom of the Serbs, Croats, and Slovenes, Yugoslavia (as it was called formally after 1929) signaled that three South Slav peoples would be considered stakeholders in the state. Officially, they were understood to be a single "three-named people," separated by historical accident but destined eventually to amalgamate again into one Yugoslav nation. This view, widespread in Serbia, was contested in both Croatia and Slovenia, where pro-Yugoslav ideology competed with ethnically based national views. Even among those sympathetic to the Yugoslav idea, however, there were differences of opinion as to how quickly the process of reconciling and perhaps eliminating "tribal" differences should go. In the political arena, the dominant Serbian parties generally insisted that other South Slavs be folded into the existing Serbian state and its institutions. The Serbs had after all been the victors in World War I, and it was logical, although ultimately destructive, for them to impose their political will on their "brothers" from defeated Austria-Hungary.

The Yugoslav political scene throughout the interwar period was characterized by a battle between Serbian wishes for a centralized, unified state and Croatian desires for a more decentralized, perhaps federal union. This began in 1921, when the new legislature adopted a centralizing constitution over the objections of Croatian parties. The situation worsened in 1929, when a constitutional crisis provoked in part by national tensions led King Aleksandar to disband parliament and declare a dictatorship; worsened again in 1934, when Aleksandar was assassinated by a Macedonian gunman assisted by the fascist Croatian Ustaša movement; and again during World War II, when, with active outside assistance, the country split apart. If politics was fractured by nationalist tension, however, the cultural arena of interwar Yugoslavia was dominated by figures who strove to create a multicultural Yugoslav nation that would synthesize elements taken from each of the separate South Slavic peoples. These included such figures as the Croatian artist Ivan Meštrović, whose most celebrated work melded a Catholic and Western sculptural plasticity to traditional Serbian themes, and the Bosnian-born writer Ivo Andrić, a future Nobel prize winner.

Even had the integration of the three partner nations been smooth, some 20 percent of Yugoslavia's population of 12 million consisted of non–South Slav minorities, including large numbers of Germans, Hungarians, Albanians, Romanians, Turks, Czechs, and Slovaks. And even the category of South Slavs was more diverse than the census figures imply, because Macedonians and Muslim speakers of Serbo-Croatian were lumped into the Serbian or Croatian population, though neither group fit comfortably into those categories. Finally, although universal manhood suffrage was introduced in 1920, women did not have the right to vote and were thus in an officially subordinate position. In this, Yugoslavia did not differ from its Balkan neighbors, none of which extended universal suffrage to women until after World War II (as was the case in most Western Europe states as well).

In addition to difficulties in achieving national integration, the interwar Balkan states faced similar economic problems. Through the late 1930s, the overwhelming proportion of the population remained dependent on agriculture. Albania was the least developed, with perhaps 90 percent of its citizens involved in farming, but the percentages for other Balkan countries were not much different, with some 80 percent of the populations in Bulgaria, Romania, and Yugoslavia and close to 60 percent in Greece working the land on small inefficient holdings. By contrast, in the same period, the comparable figures for Germany and England were 20 percent and 5 percent, respectively. To mollify their peasant populations, the Balkan countries all engaged in land-reform programs after the war, distributing large parcels that had belonged to a variety of landholders and creating small independent farms. Though this reduced the likelihood of peasant unrest, land redistribution failed to create rural prosperity. Rather, a combination of a rural population that was by most estimates 25 to 35 percent larger than necessary and low productivity (caused by lack of sufficient capital for investment in machinery and the inherent inefficiencies of small farms) conspired to keep peasant populations miserable. The worldwide collapse of prices for foodstuffs in the wake of the depression of 1929 only exacerbated an already dire situation. And strict postwar immigration quotas in the United States cut off escape routes that had existed before 1914.

Balkan governments understood the economic dangers of an over-reliance on agriculture and hoped to stimulate industrial development. Had they succeeded, surplus labor would have been drawn to towns and cities, simultaneously solving the problem of rural overpopulation, creating larger domestic markets and hence higher prices for agricultural goods, and producing more finished goods for export. The policies of successive Romanian governments illustrate what was done in this area and why it did not succeed. Even before the war, Romania had been a leading European producer of petroleum products. The expanded Romanian state acquired, in Transylvania, rich mines and a reasonable industrial base. The Liberals who governed the country between 1922 and 1928 took a number of steps to encourage further industrial development. Distrusting foreign capital, they raised domestic revenues to subsidize their industrialization program, imposing heavy tariffs on imported goods as well as large export duties on agricultural products, and invested strategically in the petroleum, food processing, textile, and mining industries. They achieved some success, especially in heavy industry. Between 1913 and 1938, Romania's index of manufacturing production rose by almost 80 percent, though it had admittedly started at a low level. The costs, however, were high and were borne primarily by an increasingly impoverished rural population. The number of Romanians employed in industry more than doubled between 1926 and 1938, but the number of new industrial jobs was barely sufficient to keep pace with the country's population increase.

Interwar Balkan governments attempted to attract foreign buyers and investment in a variety of ways. The advertisements that appeared in this special number of the Central European Review (undated, but from the late 1920s or early 1930s) are typical of such efforts. Author's collection.

The oilfields at Ploesti were a major source of export wealth for Romania. This 1934 photograph shows a Romanian soldier standing guard by the wells. National Geographic.

Other countries in the region were more friendly to outside investment. In principle, foreign capital should have allowed industrialization to proceed with less pain to local peasant populations. Foreign investors, however, demanded and frequently received generous subsidies in exchange for their Balkan ventures. They also tended to focus on industries that could produce profits quickly, concentrationg on the production of partially finished goods (agricultural and metallurgical) that could be exported for final finishing in Western Europe. In short, European investors treated the Balkans as a semicolonial region, to be exploited primarily for raw materials. And by the early 1930s, as a result of the depression, foreign investment capital all but dried up.

Ultimately, whether driven by domestic or foreign capital, the rise in industrial production in the interwar Balkan states was inadequate to siphon off excess rural populations and create a self-sustaining industrial expansion. Despite government efforts, large percentages of the population stayed in the agricultural sector and urban populations remained tiny. In 1931, for example, Yugoslavia could boast of only eleven cities with populations of more than fifty thousand, and taken together, they accounted for less than 9 percent of the country's population. With nowhere to go, farming families clung to plots that tended to become ever smaller, and farmers themselves fell into debt to banks, credit societies, and usurious local entrepeneurs. Although outright starvation was rare, rural diets were meager and consisted primarily of breadstuffs, with consumption of meat, dairy products, fruits, and vegetables far below levels in Western Europe.

By the late 1920s, all the Balkan states were experiencing political crisis. This was nowhere more obvious than in Yugoslavia, where in 1928 a parliamentary delegate from Montenegro assassinated Stjepan Radić, the popular leader of the Croatian Peasant Party, on the Parliament floor. King Aleksandar then dismissed Parliament in January 1929 and instituted a royal dictatorship. But Yugoslavia was not an exception. The turn from parliamentary government to dictatorship in the interwar period was typical in Europe, with the takeover of Italy in 1923 by Mussolini and his fascists providing a tempting model. The justifications for dictatorship were similar everywhere: first, parliamentary democracy was perceived as unworkable because of the constant infighting of political parties, and second, communism constituted a real or imagined threat. Ahmet Zogu declared himself King Zog in Albania in 1928, while in Romania King Carol, whose rule began in 1930, officially became dictator by the end of the decade. Bulgaria was under military and royal dictatorship between 1934 and 1939, and in Greece, after major electoral gains by the communists, General Ioannos Metaxas organized a right-wing coup in 1936.

Although the political, social, and economic situation of the Balkans from the late 1920s until the outbreak of World War II was difficult and chaotic, cultural life flourished. With the exception of Albania, where limited educational opportunities retarded cultural development, the art and literature of the Balkan countries in this period were heavily influenced by European modernism. Nevertheless, a synthesis of modernism with local traditions produced work that is both distinctively Balkan and a major contribution to world culture. This was true regardless of whether a given artist immigrated to Western Europe (as did the Romanian-born sculptor Constantin Brancusi), worked extensively in Europe as a diplomat (as did Ivo Andrić and the Greek poet George Seferis, both of whom would later win Nobel Prizes), or remained in his or her native land. The most extensive efforts to articulate a particular Balkan contribution to Western European modernist culture came from Ljubomir Micić, whose avant-garde "Zenit" movement operated first in Zagreb and then in Belgrade in the 1920s. Micić argued for a "Balkanization" of decadent Europe to be led by what he called the Serbian barbarogenius. In so doing, he continued a line of thinking about the power of "virile" Balkan art that had begun with the European fad for the sculpture of Meštrović.

Modern architecture flourished in the expanding Balkan capitals, and governments promoted these structures as visual emblems of their aspirations to modernity. At the turn of the twentieth century, the emphasis in much of the region was on reclaiming a Byzantine identity, illustrated by Sofia's imposing multidomed Alexander Nevsky Cathedral. International styles such as Art Nouveau and Art Deco also made their mark on the urban landscape. Here, too, the most interesting examples (such as the public baths in Sofia) display a creative mixing of local and international styles. In the 1920s, Balkan architects, alone or in collaboration with Western European partners, had actively joined the modernist movement, producing buildings that transformed the face of Belgrade, Bucharest, Ljubljana, Sofia, and Zagreb, adding multistoried modernist buildings to skylines that had been dominated by Viennese-inspired palaces.

By the late 1930s, the danger posed by Nazi Germany and fascist Italy was clear throughout Europe. Italy had the most obvious interests in the Balkans, and in the second half of the 1920s, it began to bring Albania within its orbit. By the 1930s, Italian influence was pervasive in all spheres of life and, despite the increasingly desperate efforts of King Zog, the country effectively became an Italian possession. The other Balkan states, with more room to maneuver in the 1930s, attempted to countervail the growing strength of their aggressive neighbors by creating a mutual alliance. Belying their fractious reputation, Greece, Turkey, Romania, and Yugoslavia worked closely together throughout the first half of the 1930s. Bulgaria, still aggrieved by the loss of Macedonia, refused to join them, however. Still, by 1937 it had become clear that the small states of Central Europe and the Balkans could not defend themselves in the face of ever increasing German and Italian power, even though they were spending an inordinate amount of their budget on the military. External pressure was as much economic as military, for the economies of the region became ever more dependent on that of Nazi Germany, the leading trading partner for all the Balkan states by the late 1930s.

When World War II began in 1939, the Balkan countries initially hoped to remain neutral, but this proved impossible. A pawn in the hands of Germany and the Soviet Union, Romania was forced to cede almost one third of its territory to the Soviet Union, Hungary, and Bulgaria in 1940. Dissatisfaction with this turn of events led to the creation of a right-wing dictatorship under the leadership of the Iron Guardist General Ion Antonescu. Fighting did not come to the Balkans, however, until late 1940, when the Italians decided to invade Greece. This proved a momentous mistake. The Greeks routed the Italian forces, and Hitler recognized that he could not afford to leave the region alone if he intended to invade the Soviet Union. Operation Marita, a lightning strike directed primarily against Yugoslavia and Greece in April and May of 1941, was designed to protect the German southern and eastern flank. The two countries capitulated quickly, but fierce guerrilla resistance from Greek and Yugoslav partisans tied down large numbers of German and Italian troops.

During the war years, those Balkan states that were satellites of the Germans and Italians—Bulgaria, Romania, Albania—suffered relatively little damage. Greece and Yugoslavia were not so fortunate. Yugoslavia was partitioned among Italy, Hungary, Bulgaria, and Germany. The Germans also sponsored the creation of the so-called Independent State of Croatia (Nezavisna Država Hrvatska, or NDH), a puppet state under the leadership of Ustaša strongman Ante Pavelić. The occupying forces treated the civilian populations brutally and actively encouraged interethnic violence among the Yugoslavs. By war's end, Yugoslavia had lost more than a million people (some 7 percent of the prewar population), approximately half of whom were killed by fellow Yugoslavs. The Croatian entity NDH was particularly horrible, murdering more than one hundred thousand Serbs, as well as thousands of Roma and Jews, many in the notorious concentration camp of Jasenovac. The brutality of the occupation and of the Ustaša thugs led swiftly to the appearance of resistance movements, particularly the communist partisans under the flamboyant Josip Broz (known as Tito). Although the partisans were an avowedly multinational force, toward the end of the war, they engaged in extensive retributory killings of fellow Yugoslavs accused of collaborating with the enemy, particularly in Croatia and Slovenia.

Violence during the war in Yugoslavia occurred primarily along ethnic lines, but ethnicity was not the only factor. For the war years brought to the surface enormous rifts in each of the Balkan countries between conservative and nationalist elements, on the one hand, and communists or communist sympathizers on the other. This was true even in mono-ethnic Greece, where both groups fought to rid their country of outsiders before turning on each other. It is difficult to gauge the strength of communist parties in the Balkans in the interwar period, because all were banned after initial electoral successes. During World War II, however, communist-led movements became the most significant organizers

Croatian leader Ante Pavelić traveled to Austria to be congratulated by Adolf Hitler soon after the promulgation of the puppet Independent State of Croatia. United States Holocaust Memorial Museum.

of resistance in Yugoslavia, Greece, and Albania, while playing a minor role in Bulgaria and Romania.

World War II also dealt a death-blow to Jewish communities in most of the Balkans, with Greece and Yugoslavia losing between 75 to 80 percent of their Jewish citizens and Romania at least half. The destruction of the Jews of Salonika, long a center of Jewish life in the Balkans, was particularly tragic. Though the community had been weakened significantly by the fires that destroyed most of the city during World War I, some 50,000 Jews were still living there at the beginning of World War II. Practically all had been deported to death camps by 1943. The only Jewish community in the Balkans to survive the war intact was in Bulgaria, where the government resisted German demands to deport Jews. They did, however, permit the Jews in their zones of Macedonia and Thrace to be deported, and the Bulgarian Jewish community itself would be effectively hounded out of the country after 1948.

Even as savage fighting continued throughout Europe, the postwar fate of the Balkan states was being decided at the Yalta Conference in February 1945. Behaving much like the great powers of the nineteenth century, Winston Churchill, Franklin Roosevelt, and Joseph Stalin agreed to divide Eastern Europe into spheres of influence that roughly corresponded to the military realities at the time. In the Balkans, Greece was to be part of the British and American sphere, Bulgaria and Romania (by this time already in the hands of the Soviet Red Army) were to be controlled by the Soviet Union, and Yugoslavia was to be split.

The Soviets moved quickly to assert control over both Bulgaria and Romania after the war. Leaders hand-picked by Stalin were airlifted in, and with Soviet help they consolidated communist control. Although elections were duly held as a sop to Britain and the United States, voter intimidation and outright fraud ensured enormous victory margins for the communists. The muscle of the Soviet Army and a rapidly created local secret police allowed Bulgarian and Romanian communists to eliminate all internal political opposition by 1947. Opposition figures were exiled, murdered, or sentenced to long prison terms, private property was nationalized, and communist party officials occupied all positions of political importance. As in the Soviet Union, the new states attempted to control all aspects of its citizens' lives, promising in return to benefit the working class, raise living standards, eliminate class and gender inequality, and develop the human and industrial resources of their countries. The perceived failures of interwar democratic governments, the appeal of the rhetoric of social equality, and the prestige and power of the victorious Soviet Union guaranteed the communists some support. But their brutal campaigns to eliminate opposition and the repressive methods they employed to remake society led to resentment and eventual resistance among the population. Their widespread unpopularity grew over time as promised social benefits failed to materialize, but the communists in Bulgaria and Romania would retain their hold on power until 1989.

In Greece, the situation was the reverse. The communist-led National Liberation Front (Ethniko Apeleftherotiko Metopo, or EAM) had played the leading role in the antifascist resistance. After the war, however, with the blessing of Britain and the United States, EAM was frozen out of any significant political role. Therefore, in 1945, EAM, with Tito's support, began a civil war against the right-wing government. The Soviets, satisfied with a postwar Balkan solution that gave them control over most of the region, refused to intervene, and by 1948 the Greek communists were crushed. Although postwar Greek governments were not quite as brutal as their communist counterparts, they used fear of communism as a pretext to execute some and imprison thousands of other leftists and to hound into exile many of Greece's most notable cultural figures, including the poet Yannis Rytsos, composer Mikos Theodorakis, and actress/activist Melina Mercuri. This was particularly true during a military dictatorship that lasted from 1967 to 1974. Thereafter, under the leadership of Constantine Karamanlis, Greece began to escape from the traumas of the war period. By 1981 it had become a well-functioning parliamentary democracy and joined the European Union.

In Yugoslavia, the postwar situation was perhaps most complicated. The communist-led partisans had succeeded in liberating their country with little direct Soviet military assistance. They were the most popular political force in the country, the only one with a nationwide following. Their slogan of "brotherhood and unity" was appealing in what would now be the only remaining multiethnic Balkan country. Equally important was their message of gender equality, backed by the prominent wartime role of women partisan fighters. Like his Bulgarian and Romanian counterparts, Tito had been educated in the Soviet Union and he, too, moved quickly to centralize power in the hands of the communists. Although Yugoslavia split with the Soviet Union in 1948 and slowly moved down a more independent path, the communists would remain the only political force in Yugoslavia until the end of the 1980s.

Finally, with the help of Yugoslavia, a communist regime was installed in Albania under the leadership of the xenophobic Enver Hoxha. Geographically distant from the Soviet Union, Albania had a free hand to develop into a bizarre, almost completely isolated country, retaining a Stalinist political structure until the late 1980s. The following passage from an Albanian-published book from the middle years of the Hoxha dictatorship provides a flavor for the cults of personality that most communist states built around their leadership.

[Hoxha] is the founder of the PLA [Albanian Communist Party] and has led it through all the historical stages of the revolution. He has made the greatest contribution to working out its Marxist-Leninist revolutionary line. With his wisdom, determination, foresight and revolutionary courage, Comrade Enver Hoxha has ensured the consistent, revolutionary implementation of the Marxist-Leninst line and norms of the Party, has never allowed it to be diverted on to blind alleys and has brought it triumphant through all the difficult and complicated situations. In all his works, Comrade Enver Hoxha has made a Marxist-Leninist summing-up of the revolutionary experience of the PLA, thus making an invaluable contribution to the treasury of Marxism-Leninism.

Enver Hoxha is the most beloved teacher and leader of the whole Albanian people, united in steel-like unity around the Party and its Central Committee.[2]

Most accounts of postwar Balkan developments written during the Cold War era focused on political oppression in communist Albania, Bulgaria, Romania, and Yugoslavia, as well as under the right-wing regimes in Greece. Indeed, the elimination of political dissent was a key feature of all of these societies, with show trials of dissidents and the imprisonment of thousands of real or imagined state enemies standard practice throughout the region. Under the Stalinist-style dictatorships of Albania, Bulgaria, and Romania, and to a lesser extent in Yugoslavia, the state also took almost complete control over the economy. With the exception of Yugoslavia, the governments of each of these states pursued a policy of national consolidation, consigning citizens not of the main ethnic group to second-class status. Simultaneously, for all their cruelty, these regimes partially achieved what had eluded their interwar predecessors: they eliminated many of the obstacles that had prevented their countries from reaching a Western European level of development.

In a much more committed fashion than their predecessors, communist governments attempted to reduce rural populations and their dependence on agriculture, develop heavy industry, and create an urban and literate workforce. In Yugoslavia, for example, by 1981 there were fifty-one cities with populations of more than fifty thousand (up from eleven in 1931), and they were inhabited by 41 percent of the population. Whereas 75 percent of the country had been dependent on agriculture in 1938, that percentage had fallen to approximately 50 percent by 1961. Belgrade, the capital, saw its population jump from 350,000 in 1950 to more than a million in 1989. Sofia, Bulgaria's capital, was almost the same size and had grown almost as much during this time, while Bucharest swelled to almost 2 million. Albania, whose urban population was negligible in the interwar period, could boast one of some 30 percent by 1961.

Literacy rates increased enormously throughout the region and approached 100 percent by the 1970s. Gender relations also changed substantially in the postwar communist states. Women gained the right to vote and became, in principle, equal partners of men in the workplace and political arena. In practice, however, women were usually shunted into low-paying and low-status jobs, and few reached positions of real authority. Simultaneously, they remained responsible for maintaining the family, as communist promises of state assistance for cooking, cleaning, and daycare often failed to materialize.

In Bulgaria and Romania, modernization took place under the aegis of models imported from the Soviet Union. The economy was nationalized, peasant small holders were forced onto collective farms, and surplus capital was diverted to the central government to be reinvested in industrialization. For example, in 1950, 88 percent of Romania's land was held privately. By 1960 that figure had been reduced to less than 16 percent and to less than 5 percent by 1970. As land was collectivized, surplus agricultural laborers were encouraged (sometimes compelled) to take up new occupations in the industrial sector, particularly in heavy industry, which was favored for state investment over the production of consumer goods and services. This transition was carried out at dizzying speed, and the inability of any forces in society to resist it confirms the high level of control that the communists were able to achieve, often by violent means.

Measured in terms of gross output, industrial growth in communist states, especially in the late 1950s and through the 1960s, was impressive. Bulgaria's industrial output, for example, grew in double digits for much of the 1960s. Nevertheless, rapid growth concealed major problems. In the rush to increase output at all costs, measures of profit and loss were ignored. The quality of industrial production was generally

Romanian dictator Nicolae Ceaușescu (center) makes a so-called working visit to a model collective farm. The photograph was published in a propaganda book published by the Romanian state. From Nicolae Ceaușescu: Builder of Modern Romania and International Statesman, *Oxford: Elsevier [Pergamon Press], 1983, 106.*

low and uncompetitive in world markets. Goods were instead meant for export to other communist countries. Simultaneously, communist states ignored the ecological consequences of industrialization, leading to a degradation of the environment. Finally, though it was all very well to produce enormous quantities of pig iron, increasingly urbanized populations wanted such mundane items as clothing, shoes, furniture, and other consumer goods that an economy focused on heavy industry could not provide. The state-run economy's inability to meet the basic needs of its citizens led to increasing dissatisfaction and a burgeoning black market.

Indicators of development in Bulgaria provide a snapshot of the rapid change in the economic structure of society during the communist period. In 1948, industry employed some 8 percent of the Bulgarian work force, while 82 percent of jobs were in the agricultural sector. By 1983, agriculture accounted for only 22 percent of jobs, while industry saw its share increase to 36 percent. Jobs in the transportation and service sectors grew from a combined 8 percent in 1948 to almost 33 percent in 1983. An enormous transformation had occurred in the day-to-day lives of the majority of Bulgarians in a single generation. From farmers struggling to make a living on small private plots, most Bulgarians had become urban or suburban dwellers struggling to make a living on salaries that were paid by the government, virtually the sole employer in a socialist economy.

Along with modernization, all the Balkan states except Yugoslavia pursued projects of national consolidation in the postwar years. The elimination of diversity had already begun during the war years. The Nazi death camps claimed an enormous toll of Jews and, to a lesser extent, Gypsies. Thus, although Jews had made up some 5 percent of Romania's prewar population, they made up 2 percent by 1945. Continued anti-Semitic propaganda in communist Romania caused most of the rest to flee when they were given the opportunity to emigrate to Israel after 1968. By 1977, barely 25,000 Jews remained. But it was not only minorities marked for extermination whose presence was sharply reduced in the Balkan states. In another instance of consolidation, when Romania was forced to cede northern Dobrudja to Bulgaria in 1940, a population transfer was arranged whereby some 100,000 Romanians were compelled to move north to Romanian territory while some 61,000 Bulgarians were transferred in the opposite direction. In the aftermath of the war, Germans were expelled in large numbers throughout the region. In Yugoslavia, where many Germans had actively assisted the Nazis, almost the entire prewar population of half a million was expelled.

National consolidation was also achieved by other measures. In Bulgaria, for example, state policy restricted abortion among Bulgarian women, while encouraging it among Turks and Gypsies in an attempt to reduce their numbers. Simultaneously, in discussions of Bulgarian history, emphasis was laid on the claim that the Bulgarian Turks were not actually ethnic Turks but Bulgarians who had converted to Islam and been "Turkified" during the Ottoman period. From here it was only a short step to compelling these people to take Bulgarian names (which happened in the 1980s) and forcing those unwilling to do so to immigrate to Turkey. In Albania there had never been significant minority populations, but Albanians did belong to three different religions. In the communist period, national homogenization in Albania was pursued through an almost complete ban on religion.

Educational systems played an important role as well in these consolidation efforts. In most Balkan states, textbooks and school programs from the elementary levels to universities emphasized the unity of the nation and its history, marginalizing the contributions of others to its culture. Efforts were made at every level, from policies in Greece that required restaurants to call coffee "Greek" rather than "Turkish" to the Romanian embrace of a theory that claimed many European cultural developments had in fact been invented by Romanians. As a result of such projects, by the 1980s most Balkan countries had eliminated much of their traditional diversity.

In addition, the Balkan countries during this period, again with the exception of Yugoslavia, also lost their traditional position as borderlands, although they remained peripheral areas as far as the major powers were concerned. Greece moved firmly into the Western camp as a member of the NATO alliance and later of the European Union. Bulgaria and Romania were firmly Soviet satellites, even if Romania pursued an unpredictable foreign policy under the mercurial dictator Nicolae Ceauşescu.

In terms of modernization (with all it entailed, including urbanization, industrialization, and promotion of literacy), Yugoslavia developed like its Balkan neighbors, but it differed in two significant ways. First, communist Yugoslavia chose not to pursue a program of national consolidation (that is, they did not actively attempt to create a Yugoslav nation), and after 1948, it remained a borderland, the only European country not entirely part of the Eastern or Western Bloc. Yugoslavia, therefore, was the only Balkan country to remain "Balkan" throughout the communist period.

The communist-led government that came to power in Yugoslavia in the aftermath of World War II was well aware of the savage internal

Communist states made great efforts to indoctrinate the youth in the spirit of communism. "Pioneer" organizations (state-sponsored and more or less mandatory versions of the Boy and Girl Scouts) were expected to turn out on various state holidays. Here, children march on May 24, a holiday invented by the Bulgarian communist state (and still celebrated today) called the Day of Slav Letters. Not coincidentally, this holiday takes place on the traditional date for the Bulgarian Orthodox Church celebration of the Saints Day for Cyril and Methodius. Students carry large placards with stylized Slavic letters, and in the background is a suitably secularized "icon" of the two saints whom the communist state recast as proto-Bulgarian nationalists. From Bulgaria: Twenty Years of Socialist Construction, Sofia: State Publishing House "Naouka i Izkoustvo," 1965.

fighting that had claimed half of the total casualties sustained among Yugoslavs. The new leaders believed that the roots of this conflict lay in the failure of the Serb-dominated interwar Yugoslav state to manage ethnic relations. Tito and his followers were not about to repeat those mistakes, but neither were they prepared to give up central control over the country. Their solution was the creation of a federal system (as enshrined in the 1946 constitution), in which equal rights were theoretically vested in six national republics (Croatia, Slovenia, Montenegro,

Macedonia, Bosnia-Herzegovina, and Serbia), each (except for Bosnia-Herzegovina) with its own "constituent nation." Other ethnic groups were termed "nationalities" with their own rights. But control was assured by reserving true political power in the country for the Communist party. In the immediate postwar period, the Titoist government was quite popular, and young Yugoslavs lent enormous energy to the process of postwar rebuilding.

Regarding the "national question," the new government claimed to stand for "the brotherhood and unity of the peoples of Yugoslavia." This phrase replaced an interwar locution according to which the Serbs, Croats, and Slovenes were a single "three-named people." The new use of a plural "peoples" rather than "people" implied a recognition of and tolerance for diversity. The "peoples of Yugoslavia" were undoubtedly a more diverse group than the three nations who had been the only recognized Yugoslavs between the wars. Yugoslavs now expanded to include Macedonians, and in the early 1960s, the category was expanded further with the recognition of the Bosnian Muslims as a national group. Nevertheless, Yugoslavia still contained significant non-Slavic populations, in particular the Kosovar Albanians, who occupied an ambiguous position in an avowedly South Slav state.

As the Yugoslav leaders felt the danger of both Soviet and Western interference lessen in the course of the 1950s, the government pursued a policy in which cultural, and later political, power was devolved to the various republics. The center played the role of referee and tried to encourage the mixing of national cultures, primarily through a variety of all-Yugoslav events such as film and theater festivals, book fairs and prizes, and national meetings of youth groups. Throughout the 1970s, these policies seemed remarkably successful and created conditions in which many members of the Yugoslav republics felt themselves simultaneously part of their own national culture and a pan-Yugoslavia.

In addition to nurturing a multinational and multicultural society, Yugoslavia differed from its neighbors in remaining a land in-between. In the immediate aftermath of World War II, the Yugoslav communists acted just like the other loyal satellites of the Soviet Union. They eliminated political opposition, nationalized the country's privately held enterprises, reoriented their trade toward the Soviet Union, promoted a crash industrialization program, and began to collectivize agriculture. But in 1948, primarily because of Tito's unwillingness to accept Soviet control, Yugoslavia was drummed out of the Cominform, the Soviet-sponsored organization of communist states. Initially, Tito and the leading Yugoslav communists were terrified, fearful of a Soviet invasion and concerned that Yugoslavia's economy, which was highly dependent on trade with the Soviets, would collapse. When it became apparent that no invasion was forthcoming and the split long-lasting, the Yugoslav communists began to grope their way toward what would eventually be touted as a unique version of socialism, a "third way" between Western democracy and Stalinist communism.

The concept of worker self-management, which Tito introduced in the early 1950s, was the first step in a major decentralization campaign. At around this time, Yugoslavia stopped attempting to collectivize agriculture and a few years later began to allow its citizens the right to travel and work abroad. These liberalizing trends were supported by Western countries, which were happy with the split in the communist bloc and were by 1950 already providing substantial economic aid to Yugoslavia. But Tito was no more interested in being a thrall of the West than of the East, and by the mid-1950s he mended fences with the post-Stalinist Soviet Union. From the late 1950s, Yugoslavia consciously followed a classic Balkan in-between position, and its leadership role in the international nonaligned states movement only added to its credibility.

When Ivo Andrić won the Nobel Prize for literature in 1961, a member of the Swedish Royal Academy of Sciences, G. Liljestrand, used the image of Yugoslavia as a bridge between East and West in his introduction of the writer: "Just as the bridge on the Drina brought East and West together, so your work has acted as a link, combining the culture of your country with other parts of the planet."[3] Yugoslavia's self-image as a borderland between communism and capitalism was also captured succinctly in a 1982 film entitled *Nešto izmedju* (Something in Between). Here, director Srdjan Karanović told an allegorical story about a young American journalist and her sentimental relationship with two Yugoslav men. Over the course of six weeks, the three heroes, caught in a world full of contradictions between East and West, search for their identity and appreciate the unique position of Yugoslavia.

However, Yugoslavia's delicate internal balancing between separate national and supranational cultures (between brotherhood and unity) as well as its external balancing between East and West proved unstable. By the early 1970s, the internal contradictions became stark. Demonstrations in Zagreb, driven by Croatian nationalist protests, were put down with difficulty in 1971. The 1974 constitution further decentralized the state, which essentially became a loose federation in which the separate republics followed their own self-interest rather than the collective good. What was occurring in Yugoslavia was, in effect, the same process that had occurred elsewhere in the Balkans. Traditional Balkan diversity was inexorably losing out to the Western European ideology of homogeneous nations and nation-states. Even so, when Tito died in 1980, the country survived, though its central organs became ever more enfeebled.

By the mid-1980s, communist regimes had been in place in all of the Balkan countries except Greece for almost forty years. Although certain promises had been fulfilled—illiteracy was all but eliminated, universal health care and full employment had been provided, society had become urbanized and modernized—day-to-day life under socialism was generally bleak and gray, consumer goods were scarce or available only on the thriving black market, corruption at all levels of society was endemic, the environment was degraded, and aging communist leaders were perceived to have become a "new class" ever more out of touch with the struggles of average people. Nevertheless, few would have predicted the swift disappearance of the entire system within a few years.

Indeed, this would not have happened but for changes set in motion in the Soviet Union by Mikhail Gorbachev, who became leader of the Soviet Communist party in 1985. Recognizing that the Soviet economy was on the verge of collapse, Gorbachev proposed reforms meant to allow the communists to retain political power while simultaneously opening up Soviet society in other areas. As it turned out, Gorbachev's policies opened a Pandora's box that led to the eventual collapse of the Soviet monolith. In the Balkans (as elsewhere in communist Eastern Europe), the slackening of Soviet control ushered in enormous changes. In Romania in late 1989, after the army and secret police were unable to contain mass demonstrations against the regime, a revolution led to the execution of the communist dictator Nicolae Ceauşescu and his wife, Elena. Events in Bulgaria were not as violent, but by January 1990 the communists were ousted. Though the process was less clear-cut in long-isolated Albania, monopolistic communist control was finished there as well by 1991.

The fall of the communist regimes was popular, but the first years under democratic governments were extremely difficult. It proved relatively easy for new leaders to institute political change, but the economic situation in all three countries was dire. Citizens had thought themselves badly off under socialism, but the collapse of the socialist economy and the harsh realities of the market led to a steep drop in living standards. Albania's GDP, for example, dropped by 10 percent in 1990, 28 percent in 1991, and another 7 percent in 1992, and that was from a low starting point. Inflation reached 226 percent in 1992, wiping out whatever savings the population had acquired. Though the situation was not as disastrous in Bulgaria and Romania, the same combination of GDP collapse and high inflation afflicted both countries. Economic hardship encouraged political instability. At times, conditions in all three countries were critical enough to raise fears of complete economic or political failure. Indeed, international assistance was required to stabilize Albania in 1997 when the central government disintegrated after the collapse of a financial pyramid scheme in which a large percentage of the population had invested. Nevertheless, taking advantage of their own human resources and with much prodding and help from international organizations, all three states not only survived but, by the end of the decade, all had achieved a sufficient level of political and economic stability to make it clear that they would eventually prosper.

This was emphatically not the case with Yugoslavia, which split violently into its constituent parts during the 1990s. The question of what went wrong in Yugoslavia, which a scant decade before had been seemingly the most successful of the communist states, has produced enormous controversy. The vicious wars that erupted between what remained of Yugoslavia (Serbia and Montenegro) and the newly independent state of Croatia (1991–93), inside Bosnia and Herzegovina (1992–95), and in the province of Kosovo (1999), along with more contained conflicts between Yugoslavia and Slovenia (1991) and between Slavs and Albanians in Macedonia (2001) have been blamed on everything from ancient ethnic hatreds to the actions of unscrupulous modern politicians. Commentators have cited religion, culture, demographic change, and economics as causes. All of these factors, except perhaps the first, played roles in the conflict, but perhaps the overarching issue was the multinational character of the Yugoslav state.

No matter how terrible economic conditions became, Yugoslavia's neighbors did not fall completely apart because they had all become nation-states whose citizens felt that they shared in a common enterprise. In the course of the twentieth century, each had become essentially homogeneous, marginalizing or eliminating minority populations and creating a single national culture shared by the overwhelming majority of citizens. (Bulgaria was the most diverse, but even there the population was more than 85 percent Bulgarian.) Yugoslavia, however, had attempted to preserve diversity both within the country as a whole and within its constituent parts. In many respects, this admirable commitment to multinationalism and multiculturalism made Yugoslavia a more interesting country than its Balkan counterparts. But Yugoslavia,

The city of Vukovar in eastern Slavonia was besieged by the Yugoslav National Army and Serb paramilitary forces beginning in August 1991. Although massively outnumbered by Serb forces, Croatian defenders managed to hold out until November, by which time the city had been almost completely destroyed. AP Photo/Srdjan Ilic.

even in the period from the 1950s to the 1970s, when it seemed to function well, never solved the basic contradiction between the logic of the homogeneous nation-state and the traditions of Balkan diversity.

In the early postwar days, communism was seen as an ideology that would encompass and eventually supersede the national affiliations of Yugoslavs. As power devolved from the center to the republics in the course of the 1950s and 1960s, the regime believed that granting broad cultural autonomy to the peoples of Yugoslavia would defuse desires for independent national states. This did not occur, however, as nationalist-inspired tensions grew in the 1970s. With the death of Tito in 1980, the last bonds among the peoples disintegrated. Yugoslavia did not collapse, however, until changes in external conditions occurred after 1989. With the disappearance of the Soviet Union, it was no longer possible for Yugoslavia to take advantage of a position between East and West. The end of any external threat in Europe also emboldened the smaller republics of Yugoslavia to reach for independent statehood.

In addition, the chance of being included in the European Union was an alluring prospect for some of the former Yugoslav republics.

Slovenia, whose population was more than 90 percent Slovene, could separate with relative ease. Although the Serbian leadership of the Yugoslav Army attempted in desultory fashion to prevent Slovenia's secession in 1991, they quickly realized that it was not worth the effort. In the cases of republics whose populations were mixed, however, the collapse of Yugoslavia led to a repetition of the violent homogenization that had occurred elsewhere in the Balkans. There were many who wished to continue living amid the rich ethnic diversity that had characterized Yugoslavia, but a significant portion of Yugoslavs were unwilling to accept difference. Manipulated by fear-mongering politicians, they demanded ethnically pure states and attempted to eliminate former neighbors who belonged to different ethnic, national, or religious groups.

The worst violence occurred in Bosnia. Its population consisted mostly of three groups: Bosnian Serbs made up some 34 percent; Bosnian Croatians, 18 percent; and Bosnian Muslims, 43 percent. At least in the urban areas, these three populations had gotten along quite well, but many, especially in rural areas, remained suspicious of their neighbors. Their fears were fanned by the rhetoric of most of the political parties that contested the first free Bosnian elections in 1990. Even more disastrously, Slobodan Milošević in Serbia and President Franjo Tudjman in Croatia actively supported efforts of ethnically constituted parties to break up the state. Before the shocked eyes of the world, in wars that raged through Bosnia between 1992 and 1995, Bosnian Serbs and Croats and Muslims fought bloodily. Although all three sides engaged in activities that the special UN War Crimes Tribunal for the Former Yugoslavia would subsequently find contrary to the rules of war, Bosnian Serbs, aided and abetted by what remained of the Yugoslav National Army, were clearly the initiators of the conflict and were guilty of the majority of the atrocities against civilians. Their drive to create purely Serbian territories on lands that had been characterized by diversity for hundreds of years—what came to be known as "ethnic cleansing"—culminated in the murder of some 8,000 unarmed Bosnian Muslim prisoners at Srebrenica in 1995. By the time a U.S.-led multinational coalition intervened to stop the fighting in 1995, some 100,000 Bosnians had died and more than 2 million (over half of the population of the country) had become refugees.

For much of the 1990s, an uneasy quiet reigned in the province of Kosovo, where Kosovar Albanians, who made up some 90 percent of the province's population, chafed under severe repression at the hand of the Milošević regime. By the late 1990s, however, Kosovars began to abandon the passive resistance supported by their leader Ibrahim Rugova and to engage in an armed uprising led by the Kosovo Liberation Army (KLA). The KLA strategy, almost from the outset, was to attract the attention and, eventually, the intervention of the West. Through its brutal attempts to quash the insurgency, the Milošević regime played right into the KLA's hands, and the 1990s ended with a NATO-led bombing campaign against Serbia and the de facto independence of Kosovo (which became a UN protectorate).

By a stroke of bitter irony, however, the Yugoslav wars of the 1990s, which again perpetuated the concept of the Balkans as a place of ethnic violence and war, in fact marked the death throes of the region as a distinct culture. For in the aftermath of the fighting, the former Yugoslav republics became, like their neighbors, ethnically homogeneous nation-states. In a remarkably effective military campaign in 1995, Croatia retook the Krajina region (a Serbian enclave since the days of the Habsburgs where local Serbs, with the support of Belgrade, had formed a parastate in late 1990). Some 200,000 Serbs fled Croatia in the immediate aftermath of the campaign, and few have returned. And in the wake of NATO's intervention in 1999, some 100,000 Serbs left Kosovo, which became an independent state recognized by the United States and most members of the EU in 2008. The U.S.-brokered Dayton Accords, that brought the Bosnian wars to an end in 1995, created a country that, though still multinational on paper, is in fact segregated into its three constituent peoples. The same can be said for Macedonia, where Slavic and Albanian populations essentially separated after an agreement brokered by the European Union in 2001 that averted civil war in that country.

Like their Western European counterparts, the Balkan states have, for the most part, become monoethnic parliamentary democracies. Their economies are market oriented and highly urbanized, and their populations are almost entirely literate. By 2003, both Romania and Bulgaria had been welcomed into the NATO security alliance, and they joined the EU together in 2007. Both countries can now be considered well integrated into Western Europe, a goal toward which they had been striving since their creation as nation-states in the mid–nineteenth century. Although the same processes are less advanced in Albania and the Yugoslav successor states (with the exception of Slovenia, which is already both a NATO and an EU member), they will eventually follow suit. When this process is complete, probably sometime around

2015–20, the Balkans as they were understood from the late eighteenth century on will exist only as a memory preserved in the historical, artistic, and linguistic record and passed down in many rituals of everyday life. Someday perhaps, when the term *balkanization* is used to describe events in some other part of the world, it will have to be explained for the inhabitants of what is increasingly known as Southeast Europe.

Chronology

APPROX. 35,000 BCE
Appearance of Homo sapiens in Balkan
Peninsula

APPROX. 7000 BCE
Earliest evidence of sedentary settlement
in Balkans

APPROX. 3500 BCE
Indo-European speakers enter Balkans.
Appearance of important new crops (olives,
grapes)

APPROX. 2500–1450 BCE
Height of Minoan civilization on the Island
of Crete

APPROX 1600–1100 BCE
Height of Mycenaean civilization in
mainland Greece

APPROX. 500–400 BCE
Height of Classical Greek civilization
in Athens

334 BCE–323 BCE
Reign of Alexander of Macedon (the Great)

APPROX. 250 BCE–150 BCE
Rise of Roman power in the Balkans

167 BCE
Romans defeat Illyrians, control the entire
southern portion of the Balkan Peninsula

106 CE
Romans conquer Dacia (more or less today's
Romania). Largest extent of Roman Empire

305 CE
Emperor Diocletian retires to his palace in
Split, Dalmatia

330 CE
Emperor Constantine, having recently
converted to Christianity, dedicates city of
Constantinople

LATE 5TH CENTURY CE
Fall of Rome, destruction of Western Roman
Empire as political power. Eastern Roman

(Byzantine) Empire becomes the main power
in the Balkans and Eastern Mediterranean

527–565
Rule of Justinian in Constantinople.
Construction of many important monu-
ments, including Church of Hagia Sophia

6TH AND 7TH CENTURIES
Slavic tribes cross the Danube, invade the
Balkans, and settle most of the region

APPROX. 800–927
Rise of the first Bulgarian Kingdom.
At apogee under Symeon (893–927),
Bulgarian Kingdom controls most of the
Balkan Peninsula

EARLY 9TH CENTURY
First monks come to Mt. Athos (Holy
Mountain)

863
Beginning of Moravian mission of Sts. Cyril
and Methodius. Creation of Glagolitic
alphabet for writing Slavic languages

864
Bulgarian Khan Boris accepts Christianity

10TH CENTURY
Arrival of Magyars (Hungarians) into the
Carpathians and northern Balkans

910–928
Height of the medieval Croatian Kingdom
under Tomislav

930
Founding of Rila Monastery in Bulgaria

1102
Croatian Kingdom merged with Hungarian

LATE 12TH, EARLY 13TH CENTURIES
Rise of the Serbian Kingdom under Stefan
Nemanja

1204
Crusaders capture and sack Constantinople

1219
St. Sava becomes first archbishop of autocephalous Serbian Orthodox Church

1331–1355
Greatest expansion of medieval Serbian Kingdom under Stefan Dusšan

1353–1391
Greatest expansion of medieval Bosnia under Tvrtko I

1345
Ottoman Turks appear in the Balkans

1371
Ottomans victorious at Battle of Maritsa River in Bulgaria, control most of southern Balkans

1389 ST. VITUS DAY (JUNE 28)
Battle of Kosovo

1453 (MAY 29)
Ottomans under Mehmet (the Conqueror) capture Constantinople. Renamed Istanbul, it will remain the Ottoman capital until the 20th century

1444–1468
Skanderbeg leads revolts of Albanians against Ottoman rule

1456–1462
Second rule of Vlad III (the Impaler) in Wallachia

1492
Expulsion of the Jews from Spain. Many settle on Ottoman territory

MID–16TH CENTURY
Greatest extent of Ottoman expansion. Ottomans control almost the entire Balkan Peninsula

LATE 17TH CENTURY
Habsburgs retake Hungary from the Ottomans

1804
First Serbian Uprising under Karadjordje

1809–1813
Napoleonic invasion of Dalmatia, Illyrian Provinces created

1815
Second Serbian Uprising under Miloš Obrenović

1829
Ottomans recognize Serbian autonomy

1821
Greek revolt begins in Romania, spreads to Greece by mid-1820s

1828–1830
Russo-Turkish War

1830
Ottomans forced to recognize independent Greek state

1858
Wallachia and Moldavia achieve quasi-independence

1877–1878
Russo-Turkish War

1878
Treaty of San Stefano creates enormous Bulgarian state. Bulgaria diminished considerably by subsequent Treaty of Berlin and divided into three parts. Montenegro, Romania, and Serbia recognized as independent states. Austria-Hungary occupies Bosnia-Herzegovina

1903
Ilinden Uprising in Macedonia

1908
Austria-Hungary annexes Bosnia-Herzegovina. Young Turk revolt in Ottoman Empire

1912
First Balkan War. Serbia, Montenegro, Greece, and Bulgaria all gain territory at expense of Ottoman Empire. Creation of independent Albania

1913
Second Balkan War

JUNE 28, 1914
Assassination of Franz Ferdinand in Sarajevo

AUGUST 1914
Beginning of World War I

1918–1923
In aftermath of war, Austria-Hungary and Ottoman Empire disappear. Kingdom of the Serbs, Croats, and Slovenes created. Turkish republic promulgated. Romania grows at expense of Hungary. Italians seize some of Dalmatian coast

1923
Turkish forces under Atatürk defeat Greeks in Anatolia. Population exchange moves more than 1 million Greek speakers to Greece and half a million Turkish speakers to Turkey

1928
Ahmet Zogu declared King Zog of Albania

1929
Aleksandar Karadjordjević proclaims royal dictatorship, changes country's name to Yugoslavia

1936
Ioannos Metaxas becomes dictator in Greece

1938
King Carol creates royal dictatorship in Romania

1939
Italians invade Albania

1940
Italian invasion of Greece. Romania forced to cede territory of Bulgaria, Hungary, and USSR

APRIL 1941
Germans invade Yugoslavia and Greece

1941–1944
Germans, Bulgarians, and Italians in control of Balkans. Creation of Independent State of Croatia (NDH). Partisan fighting in Greece and Yugoslavia

1945
Axis driven out of Balkans. Tito's partisans consolidate control of Yugoslavia

1946–1947
Soviet-sponsored regimes take control of Romania and Bulgaria. With assistance from Tito, Enver Hoxha consolidates control over Albania

1946–1949
Greek civil war

1948
Tito-Stalin split

1980
Death of Tito

1981
Greece joins the EU

1987
Slobodan Milošević emerges as leading figure of Serbian politics

1989–1990
Communist regimes fall in Bulgaria, Romania, and Albania

1991
Croatia, Slovenia, and Macedonia declare independence from Yugoslavia

1992
Bosnia-Herzegovina declares independence

1991–1995
Wars of Yugoslav succession in Slovenia, Croatia, Bosnia-Herzegovina

1997
Albania melts down after collapse of pyramid schemes. European intervention required to stabilize country

1999
NATO invasion of Kosovo

2000–2001
Milošević forced from power, extradited to The Hague

2004
Slovenia joins the EU

2006
Montenegro becomes independent state

2007
Romania and Bulgaria join the EU

2008
Kosovo declares independence and is recognized as an independent state by the United States and most members of the EU

Notes

CHAPTER 1

1. Herodotus, *History,* Book 5, http://classics.mit.edu/Herodotus/history.5.v.html.
2. Polybius, *The Histories,* Book II, chapter 8, http://penelope.uchicago.edu/Thayer/E/Roman/Texts/Polybius/2*.html.
3. Cited in Henry Maguire, "Images of the Court," in *The Glory of Byzantium: Art and Culture of the Middle Byzantine Era, A.D. 843–1261,* ed. Helen C. Evans and William D. Wixom (New York: Metropolitan Museum of Art, 1997), 186.

CHAPTER 2

1. Quoted in Paul M. Barford, *The Early Slavs: Culture and Society in Early Medieval Eastern Europe* (London: British Museum, 2001), 61.
2. Thomas Butler, ed., *Monumenta Serbocroatica: A Bilingual Anthology of Serbian and Croatian Texts from the 12th to the 19th century* (Ann Arbor: Michigan Slavic Publications, 1980), 110.
3. Petr Dinekov, ed., "Six Days," *Iz starata b'lgarska* literature (Sofia: B'lgarski pisatel, 1969), translation by author.
4. From the Answers of Pope Nicholas I to the Questions of Boris, 866, in *Monumenta Bulgarica: A Bilingual Anthology of Bulgarian Texts from the 9th to the 19th century,* Thomas Butler, ed. (Ann Arbor: Michigan Slavic Publications, 1996), 59.
5. Mateja Matejić and Draga Milivojević, eds., *An Anthology of Medieval Serbian Literature in English* (Columbus, Ohio: Slavica, 1978), 35.
6. Image at http://www.culture.gr/2/21/218/218ci/e218ci25.html.

CHAPTER 3

1. Ogier Ghislain de Busbecq, *The Turkish Letters of Ogier Ghiselin de Busbecq, Imperial Ambassador at Constantinople, 1554–1562* (Oxford: Clarendon Press, 1927), 60–61.
2. Benjamin Braude and Bernard Lewis, eds., *Christians and Jews in the Ottoman Empire: The Functioning of a Plural Society.* 2 vols. (New York: Holmes & Meier Publishers, 1982), vol. 1, 186.
3. Richard Clogg, ed., *The Movement for Greek Independence, 1770–1821: A Collection of Documents* (New York: Barnes & Noble, 1976), 65.
4. Radu Florescu and Raymond T. Macnally, *Dracula: A Biography of Vlad the Impaler, 1431–1476* (New York: Hawthorn Books, 1973), 77.
5. Reprinted with permission from Muçi Zade, "Lord, Don't Leave Me without Coffee," in *Lightning from the Depths: An Anthology of Albanian Poetry,* edited and translated by Robert Elsie and Janice Mathie-Heck (Evanston, Ill.: Northwestern University Press, 2008), 52–53.

CHAPTER 4

1. Mrs. John Elijah Blunt, *The People of Turkey: Twenty Years' Residence among Bulgarians, Greeks, Albanians, Turks, and Armenians,* ed. Stanley Lane Poole. 2 vols. (London: J. Murray, 1878), vol. 1, 77–78.

2. Richard Clogg, ed., *The Movement for Greek Independence, 1770–1821: A Collection of Documents* (New York: Barnes & Noble, 1976), 159.

3. Clogg, 81–82.

4. Edgar Papu from http://www.mihaieminescu.ro/en/critiques/papu.htm.

5. Paisy Hilendarski, *A Slavo-Bulgarian History,* trans. Krasimir Kabakčiev (Sofia: St. Kliment Ohridski UP, 2000), 156.

6. Quoted in Nikša Stančić, "Etničnost u hrvatskom prostoru u XIX. stoljeću: od etničke za-jednice, plemičkog naroda i pokrajinskih partikularizama do hrvatske nacije," in *Etničnost i povijest,* Emil Heršak, ed. (Zagreb: Hrvatsko sociološko društvo, 1999), 119–120.

7. Olive Lodge, *Peasant Life in Jugoslavia.* (London: Seeley, Service & Co., Ltd., 1942), 98.

CHAPTER 5

1. Quoted in Constantin Iordachi, "Charisma, Religion, and Ideology: Romania's Interwar Legion of the Archangel Michael," in *Ideologies and National Identities: The Case of Twentieth-Century Southeastern Europe,* John R. Lampe and Mark Mazower, eds. (Budapest: Central European University Press, 2004), 48–49.

2. Quoted in Stephanie Schwander-Sievers and Bernd J. Fischer, eds., *Albanian Identities. Myth and History* (Bloomington: Indiana UP, 2002), 122.

3. http://nobelprize.org/nobel_prizes/literature/laureates/1961/andric-speech-e.html.

Further Reading

GENERAL HISTORIES OF THE BALKANS

Hupchick, Dennis P., and Harold E. Cox. *The Palgrave Concise Historical Atlas of the Balkans*. New York: Palgrave, 2001.

Stavrianos, L. S. *The Balkans since 1453*. New York: New York University Press, 2000.

Stoianovich, Traian. *A Study in Balkan Civilization*. New York: Knopf, 1967.

PREHISTORIC BALKANS

Bailey, Douglass W. *Balkan Prehistory: Exclusion, Incorporation and Identity*. New York: Routledge, 2000.

CLASSICAL BALKANS

Herodotus. *The Histories*. Translated by Robin Waterfield, with an introduction and notes by Carolyn Dewald. New York: Oxford University Press, 2008.

Wilkes, John. *The Illyrians*. Cambridge, Mass.: Blackwell, 1992.

BYZANTINE PERIOD

Barford, Paul M. *The Early Slavs: Culture and Society in Early Medieval Eastern Europe*. London: British Museum Press, 2001.

Evans, Helen C., and William D. Wixom, eds. *The Glory of Byzantium: Art and Culture of the Middle Byzantine Era, A.D. 843–1261*. New York: Metropolitan Museum of Art, 1997.

Fine, John V. A. Jr. *The Early Medieval Balkans*. Ann Arbor: University of Michigan Press, 1983.

———. *The Late Medieval Balkans*. Ann Arbor: University of Michigan Press, 1987.

Mango, Cyril, ed. *The Oxford History of Byzantium*. New York: Oxford University Press, 2002.

Schenker, Alexander. *The Dawn of Slavic. An Introduction to Slavic Philology*. New Haven, Conn.: Yale University Press, 1995.

Treadgold, Warren. *A History of the Byzantine State and Society*. Stanford, Calif.: Stanford University Press, 1997.

OTTOMAN PERIOD

Adanir, Fikret. "Tradition and Rural Change in Southeastern Europe during Ottoman Rule," in *The Origins of Backwardness in Eastern Europe: Economics and Politics from the Middle Ages until the Early Twentieth Century*, ed. Daniel Chirot. Berkeley: University of California Press, 1989, 131–176.

Braude, Benjamin, and Bernard Lewis, eds. *Christians and Jews in the Ottoman Empire: The Functioning of a Plural Society*. 2 vols. New York: Holmes & Meier, 1980.

Halil Inalcik, Halil, and Günsel Renda, eds. *Ottoman Civilization*. 2 vols. Ankara: Republic of Turkey, Ministry of Culture and Tourism, 2004.

Lampe, John. "Imperialist Borderlands or Capitalist Periphery? Redefining Balkan Backwardness, 1520–1914," in *The Origins of Backwardness in Eastern Europe. Economics and Politics from the Middle Ages until the Early Twentieth Century,* ed. Daniel Chirot. Berkeley: University of California Press, 1989, 177–209.

Sugar, Peter F. *Southeastern Europe under Ottoman Rule, 1354–1804.* Seattle: University of Washington Press, 1977.

Todorov, Nikolai. *The Balkan City, 1430–1900.* Seattle: University of Washington Press, 1983.

Wolff, Larry. *Venice and the Slavs. The Discovery of Dalmatia in the Age of Enlightenment.* Stanford, Calif.: Stanford University Press, 2001.

NINETEENTH- AND TWENTIETH-CENTURY BALKANS

Fischer, Bernd J., ed. *Balkan Strongmen: Dictators and Authoritarian Rulers of South Eastern Europe.* West Lafayette, Ind.: Purdue University Press, 2007.

Jelavich, Charles, and Barbara Jelavich. *The Establishment of the Balkan National States, 1804–1920.* Seattle: University of Washington Press, 1977.

Lampe, John, and Mark Mazower, eds. *Ideologies and National Identities. The Case of Twentieth-Century Southeastern Europe.* Budapest, New York: Central European University Press, 2004.

Mazower, Mark. *The Balkans: A Short History.* New York: Modern Library, 2000.

Sugar, Peter F., and Ivo J. Lederer, eds. *Nationalism in Eastern Europe.* Seattle: University of Washington Press, 1969.

Sugar, Peter F., ed. *Eastern European Nationalism in the Twentieth Century.* Lanham, Md.: American University Press, 1995.

Todorova, Maria. *Imagining the Balkans.* New York: Oxford University Press, 1997.

Verdery, Katherine. *National Ideology under Socialism: Identity and Cultural Politics in Ceausescu's Romania.* Berkeley: University of California Press, 1991.

STUDIES OF INDIVIDUAL COUNTRIES, PEOPLES, OR REGIONS

Benbassa, Esther, and Aron Rodrigue. *The Jews of the Balkans: The Judeo-Spanish Community, Fifteenth to Twentieth Centuries.* Oxford: Blackwell, 1995.

Clogg, Richard. *A Concise History of Greece.* New York: Cambridge University Press, 2002.

Clogg, Richard, ed. *The Movement for Greek Independence, 1770–1821: A Collection of Documents.* New York: Barnes & Noble, 1976.

Crampton, R. J. *A Short History of Modern Bulgaria.* New York: Cambridge University Press, 1987.

Crowe, David M., and John Kolsti, eds. *The Gypsies of Eastern Europe.* Armonk, N.Y.: M. E. Sharpe, 1991.

Dimitrov, Bojidar. *Bulgaria: Illustrated History.* Sofina: Borina, 1994.

Harris, Robin. *Dubrovnik: A History.* London: Saqi, 2003.

Huseinović, Ismet, and Džemaludin Babić. *Svjetlost Evrope u Bosni i Hercegovini* (The Light of Europe in Bosnia and Herzegovina). Sarajevo: Buybook, 2004.

Judah, Tim. *The Serbs: History, Myth & the Destruction of Yugoslavia.* New Haven, Conn.: Yale University Press, 1997.

Karakasidou, Anastasia. *Fields of Wheat, Hills of Blood: Passages to Nationhood in Greek Macedonia, 1870–1990.* Chicago: University of Chicago Press, 1997.

Malcolm, Noel. *Bosnia: A Short History.* New York: New York University Press, 1994.

Malcolm, Noel. *Kosovo: A Short History.* New York: New York University Press, 1998.

Mazower, Mark. *Salonica, City of Ghosts: Christians, Muslims and Jews, 1430–1950.* New York: Knopf, 2004.

Ramet, Sabrina. *The Three Yugoslavias: State Building and Legitimation, 1918–2005.* Bloomington: Indiana University Press, 2006.

Tanner, Marcus. *Croatia: A Nation Forged in War.* New Haven, Conn.: Yale University Press, 1997.

Trifunovska, Snežana, ed. *Former Yugoslavia through Documents: From Its Dissolution to the Peace Settlement.* Boston, Mass.: Martinus Nijhoff, 1999.

———. *Yugoslavia through Documents: From Its Creation to Its Dissolution.* Boston: Martinus Nijhoff, 1994.

Wace, A. J. B., and M. S. Thompson. *The Nomads of the Balkans: An Account of Life and Customs among the Vlachs of Northern Pindus.* 1914. Reprint, Freeport, N.Y.: Books for Libraries, 1971.

Wachtel, Andrew Baruch. *Making a Nation, Breaking a Nation: Literature and Cultural Politics in Yugoslavia.* Stanford, Calif.: Stanford University Press, 1998.

PRIMARY TEXTS: LITERARY AND CULTURAL

Butler, Thomas, ed. *Monumenta Bulgarica: A Bilingual Anthology of Bulgarian Texts from the 9th to the 19th Centuries.* Ann Arbor: Michigan Slavic Publications, 1996.

Butler, Thomas, ed. *Monumenta Serbocroatica: A Bilingual Anthology of Serbian and Croatian Texts from the 12th to the 19th Century.* Ann Arbor: Michigan Slavic Publications, 1980.

Elsie, Robert, ed. *Balkan Beauty, Balkan Blood: Modern Albanian Short Stories.* Chicago: Northwestern University Press, 2006.

Keeley, Edmund, and Philip Sherrard, eds. *Six Poets of Modern Greece.* New York: Knopf, 1961.

Web Sites

Cultural Corridors of South East Europe
www.seecorridors.eu/?w_p = 27&w_1 = 2
This site is devoted to the "cultural corridors of South East Europe." Though it is not particularly systematic and the sites are displayed as they appear along a given road, the commentaries to each site are generally good and the list of monuments is comprehensive. Thus, following the old Roman Via Egnatia, the viewer can see monuments from the Adriatic coast in Albania to Istanbul, including classical, Byzantine, and Ottoman buildings. Further links from the site often give greater detail about a given location.

Internet Medieval Sourcebook
www.fordham.edu/halsall/sbook1.html
This is an exceptionally comprehensive site for information about the Byzantine Commonwealth. Not all of it relates to the Balkans, to be sure, but there is an extraordinary wealth of translated documentary material, particularly strong on Orthodoxy.

Serbian Cultural Treasures
www.srpskoblago.org/Archives/
This site provides spectacular images from most of the major Serbian medieval monasteries. By far the best way to see the architecture and art of the Byzantine-era Balkans without going there.

Ottoman Web Site
www.osmanli700.gen.tr/english/engindex.html
An eclectic site devoted to the history of the Ottoman Empire. In addition to capsule biographies of all the Ottoman sultans, a time line, and various images of art and architecture, the site also has a curious section called "Our Selection," which provides documents related to a variety of events ranging from the Tanzimat decree of 1839 to a list of famous Armenians in the Ottoman Empire. Commentary for most of the material is lacking and the

translations are less than ideal, but it is still extremely informative.

Vassil Levski
levski.magde.info/
A privately made and maintained site devoted to Bulgarian 19th-century revolutionary Vassil Levski. An excellent compilation illustrating the cult of "national revivers" that still exists in the Balkans.

Historical Maps of the Balkans
www.lib.utexas.edu/maps/historical/history_balkans.html
A wide range of historical maps of the Balkans from ancient times to the present. Particularly useful for maps around the time of the First and Second Balkan Wars (1912–13) and for the Yugoslav conflicts of the 1990s.

Tito's Home Page
www.titoville.com/
This somewhat tongue-in-cheek tribute to Josip Broz (Tito) contains an extraordinary number of historical photos, videos, and a great deal of trivia relating to Tito's life. Most of the site is in English, though the translations are not always perfect.

Ceauşescu
http://www.ceausescu.org/
A serious site devoted to Nicolae Ceauşescu. In addition to a large collection of still photographs, the site contains some audio and video material, including a clip of the young Ceauşescu addressing the 9th Romanian Party Congress in 1965 and propaganda songs devoted to the leader (no English translation, unfortunately).

Sarajevo Survival Map 1992–1996
www.famainternational.com/map/map-ff.htm
A detailed map of the siege of Sarajevo between 1992 and 1996. The site sells a video collection documenting the siege, but the map and legend can be downloaded free of charge.

Acknowledgments

Many people helped to fill in my knowledge gaps in the area of Balkan history. At the early stages of this project, I benefited enormously from a seminar organized at the Central European University by John Lampe, who was also gracious enough to read the entire manuscript at an early stage and provide very helpful feedback. Many of the seminar participants broadened my knowledge of the Balkans as I thought through the overall conception of the book. I am particularly thankful for the intellectual rigor of Robert Austin, Mark Biondić, Maja Brkljačić, Marko Bulatović, Constantin Iordachi, Dejan Jović, and Predrag Marković. Other colleagues read larger or smaller pieces of the work and have, I am sure, saved me from many gaffes. I would like to thank in particular Paul Barford, Aleš Debeljak, Ben Frommer, Emil Heršak, Marvin Kantor, Tijana Krstić, Kaya Sahin, and Fariba Zarinebaf. In its final stages the manuscript was significantly improved on the basis of the comments provided by the two anonymous reviewers for Oxford University Press and by my friend and colleague Igor Štiks. Despite all of their assistance, I am sure that mistakes remain, however, and I take full responsibility for them. Rita Koryan provided invaluable assistance with the visual material. The staff at Oxford University Press—my editor Nancy Toff, Justin Tackett, and Keith Faivre—have ably moved the book from the manuscript to the publication stage. Finally, I would like to thank my wife, Elizabeth Calihan, and my children, Samuel, Eleanor, and Elias, who had to put up with my multiple disappearances to various parts of the Balkans. I dedicate this book to them.

Index

Page numbers in **bold** indicate illustrations.

Achilles, 16
Acropolis, 17
Adrianople (Edirne), 22, 54
Adriatic Sea, 3–5, 22, 34, 40, 72
Aegean Sea, 5, 16–18, 47
Aeschylus, 17
Agamemnon, 16
Agrarian Party (Bulgaria), 98
agriculture, 5, 31
  in Albania, 89, 104
  Black Sea steppes and, 17–18
  in Bulgaria, 104, 115
  in Byzantine Empire, 27
  in communist period, 113–115, 119
  in Greece, 104
  in Macedonia, 89
  in medieval period, 34
  in Ottoman Empire, 54, 58, 64
  prehistoric, 12, 13, 127
  in Romania, 89, 104–105, 114
  in Serbia, 89
  in Slovenia, 88
  in twentieth century, 104
  in Yugoslavia, 104, 107, 119
Albania, 4, 6, 8, 38, 72, 81, 128
  agriculture in, 89, 104
  Balkan Wars of 1912 and 1913 and, 86
  communist period in, 112, 113, 116, 129
  economy in, 120–121, 129
  Illyrians and, 20, 29
  Islam in, 53, 62, 63
  language in, 73, 78
  Ottoman Empire and, 55, 62, 63, 65
  in twentieth century, 98, 99, 107, 108,
    120–121, 129
  women in, 65
  in World War I, 91, 94
  in World War II, 109, 110
Aleksandar, King of Yugoslavia, 101, 103, 107
Aleksandar Karadjordjević, Crown Prince of
    Serbia, 92, 101, 103, 107
Alexander, Prince of Battenburg, 86
Alexander Nevsky Cathedral, Sofia, 108
Alexander of Macedon (the Great), 11, 19, 127
alphabet
  Cyrillic, 45, **46**
  Glagolitic, 45, **46**, 127
  Mycenaean, 16

Americas, opening of, 68
Anatolia, 14, 44, 51, 55, 62, 66, 69, 129
Andrić, Ivo, 1, 2, 103, 107, 119
animals, domestication of, 12, 14, 15
Antonescu, Ion, 109
architecture
  in Bulgaria, 50
  medieval, 49
  in Ottoman Empire, 69–70
  in twentieth century, 108
Aristophanes, 17
Aristotle, 17
Armenians, 62
art
  medieval, 49–50
  Minoan, 15
  Mycenaean, 16
  in twentieth century, 107–108
Art Deco, 108
Art Nouveau, 108
Asdrakhas, S. I., 60
Asia Minor, 5, 13, 56, 94
Athens, Greece, 16, 17, 69, 87, 127
Atlantis, lost city of, 15
Attica, 16
Austria-Hungary (Austro-Hungarian Empire),
    35, 53, 68, 69, 72, 74, 84, 87, 90–93, 101,
    102, 103, 128

Balkan Mountains, 1, 4
Balkan Wars of 1912 and 1913, 86, 128
banditry, 68
Bayezid I, Sultan, 56
Belgrade, Yugoslavia, 21, 22, 75, 87, 107, 108
Benedictine order, 46
Berlin, Treaty of (1878), 84, 86, 128
Bessarabia, 84, 92
Black Sea, 3–5, 14, 16–18, 34, 38
Bolshevik coup (October 1917), 92
Boris I, King of Bulgaria, 42–44, 47, 127
Boris III, King of Bulgaria, 98
Bosnia, 1, 2, 4, 9, 20, 29, 37–40, 53, 84
  ethnic cleansing in, 123
  Islam in, 53, 62, 63
  Ottoman Empire and, 55, 62, 63
  in postwar period, 118
  in twentieth century, 121, 123, 129
  women in, 65

Bosnia-Herzegovina, 118, 128, 129
Bosnian Chronicle, A (Andrić), 1
Bosphorus, 5, 16
Botev, Hristo, 80
Brancusi, Constantin, 107
Branković, Vuk, 55
Bratianu, Ion, 91, 98
Brutus, 23
Bucharest, Romania, 108, 113
Bucharest, Treaty of, 86
Bulgaria, 4, 8, 18, 29, 34, 40, 72, 127
  agriculture in, 104, 115
  art and architecture in, 50
  Balkan Wars of 1912 and 1913 and, 86, 128
  Berlin Treaty and, 84, 86, 128
  communist period in, 111, 113–116, 129
  economy in, 121
  education in, 83
  integration into Western Europe, 124
  Islam in, 53, 62
  Jews in, 110
  language in, 73
  national revival in, 79–81, 83–84
  Ottoman Empire and, 53–56, 62
  prehistoric, 11, 13–14
  religion in, 42–44, 47, 53, 62, 83
  San Stefano treaty and, 84, 128
  in twentieth century, 98, 100, 101, 107, 108, 129
  in World War I, 92, 94, 98
  in World War II, 108–110
Bulgarian gold jug, **32**
Bulgars, 3, 28, 29, 32, 34–37, 43
Bunch, Mrs. John Elijah, 74
Busbecq, Ogier Ghiselin de, 57
Byzantine Empire, 1, 3–5, 25–27, 34–37, 43, 44, 51–52, 60, 67, 75, 127
Byzantion, 23
Byzantium (Istanbul), 21

Caesar, Julius, 23
Canetti, Elias, 2
Carol, King of Romania, 107, 129
Carpathians, 17, 127
Castriot, John, 65
Catholicism, 1, 3, 4, 25, 30, 37, 42–44, 48, 51, 53, 54, 59, 62, 74
Caucasus Mountains, 4
Ceaușescu, Nicolae, **114**, 116
Celts, 5, 19
Central European Review, advertisements in, **105**
Christianity, 3, 23, 25, 28, 29–30, 35, 40–45, 127
Chrysopolis, Battle of, 23
Churchill, Winston, 110
Circassians, 62
city-states, 17
Classical Greek civilization, 16–18, 127

climate, 5
clothing, Slavic, 33
Codreanu, Corneliu Zelea, 102
coffee, 70–71
Cold War era, 113
collectivization, 113–114, 119
Cominform, 118
communism, 97, 98, 107, 111–120, 122, 129
Constantine, King of Greece, 92, 98
Constantine, Roman emperor, 23–25, 127
Constantinople, 4, 23–25, 30, 33, 36, 48, 51, 56, 61, 127, 128
corruption, in Ottoman Empire, 60–61
cremation, 32
Crete, 15, 16, 127
Croatia, 4, 29, 37, 40, 72, 74, 87, 127
  Kingdom of the Serbs, Croats, and Slovenes, 72, 92–94, 98, 103, 128
  in postwar period, 117, 119
  prehistoric, 11
  religion in, 44
  in twentieth century, 103, 121, 124, 129
  in World War II, 109
crops. *See also* agriculture
  prehistoric, 14
Crusades, 4, 25, 36, 48, 51, 127
Cyprus, 100–101
Cyril, St., 45, 47, 127
Cyrillic alphabet, 45, **46**

Dacians, 22–23, 29, 127
Dalmatia, 4, 20, 21, 88, 94, 127, 128
Dalmatos monastery, Constantinople, 46
Danube River, 5, 12, 17, 19, 23, 30, 36
Danubian Principalities, 81
Dardanelles Straits, 5, 52
Day of Slav Letters holiday, Bulgaria, **117**
Dayton Accords, 124
depression of 1929, 104
devshirme (child recruitment), 58, 59, 62
dhimma (security compact), 59
Diocletian, Roman emperor, 11, 23, 127
Dobrudja, 81, 115
Dracula (Stoker), 67
Drava River, 5
Drina River, 5
Dubrovnik, Republic of, 35, 74
Dubrovnik, Yugoslavia, 22, 33, 37, 38
Dubrovnik's trade in the mid-thirteenth century (map), **41**
Dyrrhachium (Durrës), 21

Eastern Orthodox Church, 25, 30
Eastern Roman Empire, 22
Eastern Rumelia, 84, 86
economy, 33–34, 63–64, 67–69, 87, 96, 100, 104–105, 120–121, 124, 129
Edirne, 22, 54, 61

education, 90
   in Bulgaria, 83
   in Byzantine Empire, 27
   in communist period, 116
   nation building and, 79
Egnatian Way, 21–23
Egypt, 15, 17, 74, 75
Eminescu, Mihai, 79
Emona (Ljubljana), 21, 22
Epiros, state of, 20
Ethnic cleansing, 54, 95, 123
Euripides, 17
European Union, 22, 97, 124, 129
Evans, Sir Arthur, 15

fascism, 97, 98, 100, 102, 107
Ferdinand, King of Bulgaria, 98
France, 76, 83, 92, 94
Franciscan order, 46
Franks, 43
Franz Ferdinand, Archduke, 91, 128
French Revolution of 1789, 74–75
FYROM (Former Yugoslav Republic of
   Macedonia), 19

Gaj, Ljudevit, 88
Gallipoli, 52
geography, 1, 4–5
Germany, 84
   language, 73
   national consciousness, 77
   in World War I, 91, 92
   in World War II, 98, 100, 108–109, 129
ghazis (warriors of the faith), 57
glaciation, 11
Glagolitic alphabet, 45, 46, 127
Gračanica monastery church, 50
grand viziers, 59
Great Britain, 6, 83, 84, 92, 94
Greece, 4, 8, 38, 40, 72
   agriculture in, 104
   Balkan Wars of 1912 and 1913 and, 86, 128
   classical period and, 16–18, 127
   dispute with Macedonia, 11, 19
   Islam in, 62
   language, 73, 75, 78, 83
   map of expansion of independent (1804–
      1919), 82
   Minoan civilization and, 15, 127
   Mycenaean civilization and, 16, 127
   national revival in, 79, 81–83
   Ottoman Empire and, 53, 54, 62
   in postwar period, 111–113, 116
   prehistoric, 3, 4, 11
   Slavs in, 44–45
   Turkey and, 94–95, 100–101, 129
   in twentieth century, 98, 100, 107, 108, 129
   in World War I, 92, 94
   in World War II, 4, 109, 110, 129

Greek Orthodox Church, 42–47, 51, 53, 59, 62,
   69, 83
guilds, 63, 65

Hagia Sophia (Church of Holy Wisdom), 24,
   24, 127
Hajduks, 68
"Hanging of Vassil Levski, The" (Botev), 80
Hapsburgs, 6, 53, 68, 69, 72, 74, 90, 128
Herodotus, 17, 18
Herzegovina, 4, 9, 21, 38, 53, 81, 84, 121
Hilander monastery, Mount Athos, 48, 49
History (Herodotus), 18
Hitler, Adolf, 100, 109, 110
Homer, 16
housing
   prehistoric, 12
   Slavic, 33
Hoxha, Enver, 112, 129
Hungarians, in Romania, 102
Hungary, 4, 29, 36–38, 66, 68, 91, 94, 127, 128
   in World War II, 108, 109
hunter-gatherers, 12, 13

Ice Age, 11
Iliad, The (Homer), 16
Illyrian provinces, 74–75, 128
Illyrians, 19–21, 29, 127
Illyricum, province of, 21
IMRO, 101
Independent State of Croatia (Nezavisna Država
   Hrvatska, NDH), 109, 110, 129
Indo-European tribes, 14, 127
Industrial Revolution, 68
Ionian Sea, 5
Iron Guard, 102, 109
Islam, 53, 59, 62–63
Isperikh, Bulgar chief, 36
Israel, 115
Istanbul, 51, 58, 61–63, 83, 128
Italy, 94, 100, 107–109, 128, 129

janissaries, 58, 75, 76
Jasenovac concentration camp, 109
Jefimija, 49
Jews, 8
   in Bulgaria, 110
   in Ottoman Empire, 53–54, 59, 61–63
   in Romania, 102, 115
   in Spain, 5, 53, 128
   in World War II, 110, 115
John of Ephesus, 31
John of Rila, 47, 49
John the Exarch, 36–37
Justinian, Roman emperor, 24, 127

Karadjordje (Djordje Petrović), 76, 128
Karadjordjević dynasty, 98
Karadžić, Vuk, 55–56, 78, 88

Karamanlis, Constantine, 112
Karanović, Srdjan, 119
Karanovo, Bulgaria, 13
Keyserling, Hermann, 7
Kingdom of the Serbs, Croats, and Slovenes, 72, 92–94, 98, 103, 128
Krum, Khan, 36
Klephts, 68
Kliment, St., 47
Knossos, Crete, 15
Kopitar, Jernej, 78
Kosovar Albanians, 118, 123–124
Kosovo, 6, 30, 38, 50, 69, 121, 123–124, 129
Kosovo, Battle of, 91, 128
Kosovo Liberation Army (KLA), 124
Kosovo Polje (the Field of Blackbirds), Battle of, 55
Kosovo songs, 55–56
Krajina region, 124

Ladino language, 73
Lake Ohrid, Macedonia, 30, 47, 50
Lake Shkodër, Albania, 20
"Lament for Baby Uglješa" (Jefimija), 49
land-reform programs, 104
languages, 6, 45, 73, 77–78
Latin language, 73
Lausanne, Treaty of (1923), 95
law code, 38
Lazar, Prince, 35, 55–56
Lepenski Vir, 12
Levski, Vassil, 80, 83
Liberal Party (Greece), 98
Liljestrand, G., 119
Linear A script, 15
Linear B alphabet, 16
Lion Gate, Mycenae fortress, Greece, 11, 15
literacy, 30, 42, 45–46, 90, 113
literature
    cult of national, 78–79
    in medieval period, 48–49
    in twentieth century, 107
Ljubljana, Slovenia, 21, 22, 108
Lodge, Olive, 90
"Lord, Don't Leave Me without Coffee," 70–71

Macedonia, 2, 4, 9, 18, 64, 81, 110, 128
    agriculture in, 89
    art and architecture in, 50
    Balkan Wars of 1912 and 1913 and, 86
    claims on territory of, 84, 86
    classical period and, 18–19
    dispute with Greece, 11, 19
    Ottoman Empire and, 62, 86
    in postwar period, 118
    Republic of, 19
    in twentieth century, 100, 101, 108, 121, 124, 129

Magyars (Hungarians), 5, 29, 37, 127
maps
    Balkans: geographical features and contemporary political borders, xii
    Balkans: in 7th–8th centuries, 26
    Balkans: political borders in 1923, 99
    Dubrovnik's trade in the mid-thirteenth century, 41
    expansion of independent Greece and Serbia (1804–1919), 82
    Ottoman Empire, 52
Mark Anthony, 23
market economy, 68, 98
Marsigli, Count Luigi, 64
Mažuranić, Ivan, 88
medieval period (Middle Ages), 6, 29–50, 54
Mehmet, Sultan "the Conqueror," 51, 61, 128
Mehmet Ali, 82
Mendes, Dona Gracia, 61
Mercuri, Melina, 112
Mesolithic period, 12, 13
Meštrović, Ivan, 103, 108
metalworking, 14, 17, 31
Metaxas, Ioannos, 107, 129
Methodius, St., 45, 47, 127
Michael III, Byzantine emperor, 43, 45
Micić, Ljubomir, 107–108
military, in Ottoman Empire, 57–58
Military Frontier (Krajina), 74
millet system, 59–61, 73
Milošević, Slobodan, 123, 124
Milvian Bridge, Battle of, 23
mining, 14, 34, 68, 104
Minoan civilization, 15, 17, 127
Minotaur, 15
Mircea, Prince of Wallachia, 56, 66
missionaries, 30, 43, 45
Mlada Bosna (Young Bosnia) movement, 91
modernism, in art and literature, 107
Moldavia, 56, 66, 128
Moldova, 9
monasticism, 46–47, 127
Mongolia, 4
Montenegro, 4, 6, 38, 53, 69, 72, 107, 129
    Balkan Wars of 1912 and 1913 and, 86, 128
    Islam in, 53
    in postwar period, 117, 121
Morava River, 5
Moravia, 45
Morlacchi (Dalmatian Slavs), 75
Mount Athos (Holy Mountain), 46–47, 49, 83, 127
Murad, Sultan, 54, 55
Muslims, 7, 8
    in Ottoman Empire, 57–65
    in Spain, 5
Mussolini, Benito, 100, 107
Mustafa Kemal (Atatürk), 92, 93, 129
Mustapha III, Sultan, 83

Mycenae fortress, Greece, 11, 15
Mycenaean civilization, 16, 127

Nagy-Talavera, Nicholas M., 102
Napoleon, emperor, 21, 74–75
Nasi, Don Joseph, 61
nation, concept of, 72
nation-state ideology, 7–8
national awakeners, 75, 88
national independence movements, 5, 75–77, 80–83
National Liberation Front (Ethniko Apeleftherotiko Metopo, EAM), 111
NATO (North Atlantic Treaty Organization), 97, 116, 124, 129
Naum, St., 47
Navarino, Battle of, 83
Neolithic period, 12–15
Nešto izmedju (Something in Between), 119
Nicaea, church council at, 25
Nicholas II, Tsar, 92
Noli, Bishop Fan, 99
North Africa, 16

Obilić, Miloš, 55
Obrenović, Miloš, 128
Octavian, Roman emperor, 23
Odysseus, 16
Odyssey, The (Homer), 16
Old Church Slavic language, 45, 73, 78
Olovo, 34
Operation Marita, 109
Osman, Sultan, 51
Otho, Prince of Bavaria, 83
Ottoman Empire, 1, 3–7, 25, 35, 38, 40, 48, 51–76, 80–86, 116, 128
  map of, 52
Ottoman Turkish language, 73
Ottomans, 29

paganism, 30–32, 41
Paisi, Father, 83
Parry, Milman, 97
Parthenon, Greece, 69
Pašić, Nikola, 98
Pavelić, Ante, 109, 110
Peasant Life in Jugoslavia (Lodge), 90
Peasant Party (Croatian), 107
Peloponnesus, 16, 30, 81
Philip, King of Macedonia, 18, 19
Philipopolis (Plovdiv), 21, 22
Philippi, Battle of, 23
Phoenicia, 15
piracy, 20–21, 34
Plato, 17
Pliska, Prince, 34
Ploesti oilfields, Romania, 106
political organization, 29, 35–37, 56–57, 59–60, 74, 99–104, 107

Polybius, 20
Pompei, 23
pottery
  prehistoric, 12, 13
  Slavic, 32
prehistoric period, 11–15, 127
Preslav, 34, 47
Procopius, 24
Protestantism, 25
Pula amphitheater, Croatia, 21

Radić, Stjepan, 107
Radical Party (Serbia), 98
Radu, 66
Ragusa (Dubrovnik), 22, 33, 39, 72
rainmaking ritual, 6
Ras, Prince, 34
Raška, Serbia, 38, 69
Rastko (Sava), 47–49, 128
Ratislav, King of Moravia, 45
Ravenna, Italy, 26
refugee issue, 100–101
religion, 6, 29–31, 35, 73–74
  in Bulgaria, 42–44, 47, 53, 62, 83
  Christianity, 3, 23, 25, 28, 35, 40–45, 127
  in communist period, 116
  in Croatia, 44
  Islam, 53, 59, 62–63
  in Ottoman Empire, 53, 58–63
  in Serbia, 47–48, 83
Rila Mountains, 4, 47
Rodina Magazine illustration, 85
Roma (Gypsies), 8, 29, 53, 115
Roman Catholicism, 1, 3, 4, 25, 30, 37, 42–44, 48, 51, 53, 54, 59, 62, 74
Roman Empire, 1, 3, 5, 21–24, 30, 75, 79, 127
Romania, 4, 8, 17, 23, 29, 67, 72, 81
  agriculture in, 89, 104–105, 114
  art and architecture in, 50
  Balkan Wars of 1912 and 1913 and, 86, 128
  communist period in, 111, 113–116, 129
  economy in, 121
  integration into Western Europe, 124
  Jews in, 102, 115
  language, 38
  language in, 73
  literary work in, 79
  nation building and, 79
  Ottoman Empire and, 54
  in twentieth century, 98, 101–102, 104–108, 129
  in World War I, 91–92
  in World War II, 108–110, 129
Roosevelt, Franklin, 110
Rugova, Ibrahim, 124
Russia, 9, 76, 83, 84, 92
Russo-Turkish War of 1877–78, 83–85, 128
Rytsos, Yannis, 111

St. Blaise, patron saint of Dubrovnik fresco, 40
St. Theodore icon, 49–50, **50**
Salonae (Solin), 21
Salonika, Greece, 30, 33, 45, 61, 91, 92, 110
San Stefano, Treaty of (1878), 84, 91, 101, 128
Sarajevo, Bosnia, 61, 63, **64, 70**
Sava River, 5
Saxons, 34
Scherer, Johan Krstnik, 74–75
Schleimann, Heinrich, 16
sculpture, prehistoric, 12
Scythians, 18
Seferis, George, 107
Selim II, Sultan, 59
Selim III, Sultan, 75
Serbia, 4, 17, 29, 34, 38, 40, 121, 124, 127
   agriculture in, 89
   art and architecture in, 50
   assassination of Franz Ferdinand and, 91, 128
   Balkan Wars of 1912 and 1913 and, 86, 128
   Bosnia and, 123
   Islam in, 62
   Kingdom of the Serbs, Croats, and Slovenes,
      72, 92–94, 98, 103, 128
   language in, 78
   map of expansion of independent
      (1804–1919), **82**
   migrations from, 69
   nation building and, 79, 81
   national revival in, 69, 75–76
   Ottoman Empire and, 53–55, 62, 69
   in postwar period, 118
   religion in, 47–48, 69, 83
   Russia and, 76
   in twentieth century, 98, 103, 129
   in World War I, 91, 94, 103
Serbian Orthodox Church, 48, 128
Serdica (Sofia), 21, 22
Sèvres, Treaty of (1920), 94
Sigismund I, King of Hungary, 56
Singidunum (Belgrade), 21, 22
sipahi (cavalry-men), 57
Skanderbeg, 65, 66, 128
Skoplje, Serbia, 38, 63–64
Slavic languages, 34, 44
Slavs, 3, 22, 28–36, 39, 42, 44, 45–46, 127
Slovakia, 38
Slovenes, 29
Slovenia, 74, 121
   agriculture in, 88
   Kingdom of the Serbs, Croats, and Slovenes,
      72, 92–94, 98, 103, 128
   in postwar period, 117
   in twentieth century, 103, 129
   in World War II, 109
Smyrna, 94
Socrates, 17
Sofia, Bulgaria, 21, 22, 80, 87, 108, 113
Sokollu, Mehmet Pasha, 59, 69

Sophocles, 17
Southeast Europe, 9, 125
Soviet Union
   collapse of, 122
   postwar period, 111–113, 118–119
   in World War II, 108–111
Spain, 5, 53, 128
Spalato (Split), 33
Split, Dalmatia, 11, 21–23, 33, 127
Srebrenica, Bosnia, 34, 123
Stalin, Joseph, 110, 111, 129
Stambuliski, Alexander, 98, 101
Stefan Dušan, King of Serbia, 38, 48, 51,
   54, 128
Stefan I Nemanja, King of Serbia, 38, 47–49,
   127
Stoker, Bram, 67
Studenica, Serbia, 48
Suleiman I, Sultan "the Magnificent," 59
Symeon I, King of Bulgaria, 36–37, 45, 47, 51,
   84, 127

Tamerlane, 56
Tatars, 62
technological change, prehistoric, 13–14
tells, 11, 13
Teuta, Queen of Illyria, 20–21
Theodorakis, Mikos, 111
Theodosius, Roman emperor, 24
Thessaly, Battle of, 23
Thira, 15
Thrace, 84, 89, 100, 110
Thracians, 17–19
Thucydides, 17
timar system, 57–58, 65, 68
Tirana, Albania, **87**
Tito, Marshal (Josip Broz), 109, 111, 112,
   117–120, 122, 129
Tomislav, King of Croatia, 37, 127
tools, prehistoric, 12–13
Transylvania, 17, 38, 72, 91, 92, 102, 104
*Travels in the Slavonic Provinces of Turkey-
   in-Europe* (Mackenzie and Irby), **89**
Trogir, Yugoslavia, 33
Trojan War, 15
Tudjman, Franjo, 123
Tunis, 59
Turkey, 1, 4, 9, 72, 128. *See also* Ottoman
   Empire
   birth of modern, 92
   Greece and, 94–95, 100–101, 129
   in twentieth century, 108, 129
Turkic dialect, 36
Turkish refugees (1913), **95**
Tvrtko I, King of Bosnia, 38, 128

Ukraine, 4, 9, 38
United Nations War Crimes Tribunal, 123

universal suffrage, 104
University of Zagreb, 90
Upper Paleolithic period, 11
Ustaša movement, 103, 109

vampires, 67
Vardar River, 5
Varna, Bulgaria, 87
Velestinlis, Rhigas, 75
Venetians, 36, 51, 72, 74
Venizelos, Eleutherios, 92, 98, 100
Vergina, Macedonia, 19
Via Egnatia, 21–23
Vlachs, 8, 23, 29, 39, 53, 62
Vlad II, 66
Vlad III Dracul (Vlad the Impaler), 65, **66**,
    66–67, 128
Vladimir, King of Bulgaria, 47
Vojvodina, 69, 72
Vukovar, Slavonia, **122**

Wallachia, 38, 55, 56, 65–67, 128
warrior graves, 14
weapons, 14, 17
women
    in Ottoman Empire, 64–65
    in postwar period, 113

worker self-management, concept of, 119
World War I, 53, 84, 91–93, 98, 103, 128
World War II, 4, 98, 100, 103, 108–110, 115,
    129

Yakub, Hekim, 61
Yalta Conference of 1945, 110–111
Yemen, 59
Ypsilantis, Alexander, 81
Yugoslavia, 91, 92
    agriculture in, 104, 107, 119
    collapse of, 8, 97
    communist period in, 112, 113,
        115–122
    in twentieth century, 100, 101, 103–104,
        106–108, 129
    in World War II, 4, 103, 109–110,
        115, 129
Yürüks, 62

Zadar, Croatia, 22, 33, 38
Zagreb, Croatia, 87, 107, 108, 119
Zalikoglou, Grigoris, 77–78
Zenit movement, 107
Zeta, principality of, 38, 48, 69
Zogu, Ahmet (King Zog), 99, 107,
    108, 129

Andrew Baruch Wachtel graduated
from Harvard College in 1981 and
went on to pursue doctoral studies
in Slavic languages and literatures at
the University of California, Berkeley,
where he received his Ph.D. in 1987.
A wide-ranging scholar, his interests
have always focused on the complex
interrelationship between history and
culture. In addition to academic writing
on topics in Russian, Balkan, and East
European studies, Wachtel is active as a
translator of poetry and prose and as a
publisher of literary work from Eastern
Europe in English translation. Married
to Elizabeth Calihan, a psychiatrist, he
lives with her and their three children in
Evanston, Illinois, where he is dean of
the Graduate School at Northwestern
University.

The
New
Oxford
World
History

Forthcoming Titles

CHRONOLOGICAL VOLUMES

The World from 4000 to 1000 BCE
The World from 1000 BCE to 300/500 CE
The World from 300 to 1000 CE
The World from 1000 to 1500
The World from 1450 to 1700
The World in the Eighteenth Century
The World in the Nineteenth Century
The World in the Twentieth Century

THEMATIC AND TOPICAL VOLUMES

The City: A World History
Democracy: A World History
Empires: A World History
The Family: A World History
Race: A World History
Technology: A World History

GEOGRAPHICAL VOLUMES

China in World History
Russia in World History
The Silk Road in World History
South Africa in World History
South Asia in World History
Southeast Asia in World History

Printed in Australia
AUHW011454131219
321294AU00004B/14